KendallHunt
publishing company

BEYOND STRESS
Strategies for blissful living

Maria Napoli

Dr. Maria Napoli is Associate Professor at the Arizona State University, Director, Integrative Health Initiative. She has incorporated the practice of mindfulness in research, teaching, trainings and presented at conferences nationally and internationally. Dr. Napoli has been instrumental in developing training programs incorporating mindfulness for elementary schools and health professionals.

In addition to journal articles, she has published a family based case study book incorporating problem based learning and mindful self reflection; *Tools for Balanced Living: Steppingstones for Practice* featuring her Mindful MAC Guide, and co-authored *Life by Personal Design: Limitless Horizons*. Dr. Napoli is a certified Kripalu Yoga instructor and Phoenix Rising Yoga Therapist. She developed a Graduate Certificate in Integrative Health and Stress Management Curriculum at Arizona State University offering students, professionals, hospital personnel and community the development of mindfulness practice and extensive information in whole person health.

MEDITATION MUSIC AND VOICEOVER

Susan Busatti Giangano is a voice actress, composer and singer songwriter. She is a classically trained pianist. The piano is her primary instrument, but it is only one of many. As a member of SAG and BMI, she has written music for film. Her songs have been licensed to film and TV. To kick her songwriting into gear, she recently wrote and recorded 52 songs in 52 weeks. She has acted on camera in addition to her voiceover work. The study of yoga and taekwondo keep her busy on Long Island where she resides with her husband, two sons and her golden retriever, Teddy.

Please visit mindfulmac.com and suziegmusic.com

ISBN 978-1-5249-3415-6

9 781524 934156

00006

T2-BUW-346

Contributors

Chapter 2   The Joy of Living in the Parasympathetic System

David Berceli, Ph.D.

David Berceli, PhD, is an international author, presenter, and trainer in the areas of trauma intervention stress reduction and resiliency strengthening. He has lived and worked in war-torn countries and natural disaster zones around the world. He specializes in trauma recovery with large populations, that is, military personnel, national and international relief agencies, and government and nongovernment organizations whose staff are living and working in trauma-inducing environments. Dr. Berceli is also the creator of a revolutionary set of tension and trauma releasing exercises (TRE). David is the author of: *The Revolutionary Trauma Release Process: Transcend Your Toughest Times.* Currently he teaches trauma recovery and awareness in 30 countries and provides relief services through his nonprofit organization to survivors of natural and human made disasters around the world. www .traumaprevention.com and www.bercelifoundation.org

Chapter 3   Whole Person Health Across the Life Span

Steve Peterson, CPhT, M.Ed., MAIS

Steve Peterson, CPhT, MEd, MAIS, is associate faculty for Arizona State University's Integrative Health Initiative and has over eleven years of experience in the education sector as pharmacy program director and campus dean of education. He has also provided service as a Chemotherapy-Certified Intravenous Compounding Technician for Scottsdale Healthcare, a Level I Trauma Facility, since 1997. Steve received his postbaccalaureate certificate in Assessment of Integrative Health Modalities from Arizona State University in 2010 and earned his second master's degree in the integrative health discipline. He holds an instructor certificate in Dr. David Berceli's revolutionary trauma releasing exercises (TRE). Steve is an Advisory Board member for the Accrediting Bureau of Health Education Schools (ABHES) and one of the coauthors of the National Standards for Pharmacy Technician instructional programs. He is also currently involved in an independent research project to determine and measure if an olfactory stimulus will have an effect on patient blood pressure in a clinical setting.

Chapter 4   Sustainable Living and Conscious Eating

Lisa Schmidt, MS, CYT, e-RYT

Lisa Schmidt is an expert in the science of behavioral change, holding dual MS degrees in nutrition and clinical health psychology.

Lisa is an integrative health therapist, and works at the intersections of food, mood, and mindfulness. She is certified as a yoga teacher with the Yoga Alliance and is a registered experienced yoga instructor, specializing in trauma sensitive, functional yoga, and yoga therapy. Lisa inspires her clients to find their own healing through a holistic and integrative mind–body approach by combining nutritional, physical, spiritual, emotional, psychological, and energetic aspects of life. She is a firm believer that a healthy lifestyle and balanced diet combined with a positive sense of self is best for your body as a form of natural medicine. Lisa is a trained meditator and maintains an active yoga and mindfulness practice.

Prior to Lisa's clinical training, she held executive positions with a large health care system and was directly responsible for the health and well-being of 50,000 employees. Other corporate experience includes several years as a director of Weight Watchers International, where her innovative approach to change ignited the success of thousands of members over fourteen years.

Lisa's business, Lisa Schmidt Counseling, LLC is devoted to improving individuals' health and wellness, one client at a time. You can read more about this integrative approach to health and wellness at Lisa Schmidt Counseling. (http://www.lisaschmidtcounseling.com)

Chapter 5   Impact of Global Environmental Stress on Universal Well-Being: Be the Solution

Patricia Duryea, PhD

Patricia Duryea, PhD, has a diverse background including: medical technology, human resources, small business owner, and mental health counseling.

Pat is the owner of Duryea and Associates which provides wellness consulting and counseling. Part-time, Pat is an adjunct professor at Webster University and Arizona State University. She is also a Heart Math provider for stress reduction.

Chapter 6   The Science of Instincts and Intuition: Intuitive Smartness in Times of Information Overload

Jonas Nordstrom, PhD, MSc, is an international trainer and lecturer in the field of stress reduction and trauma recovery. He has lived and worked in war-torn countries like Afghanistan, Kosovo, Israel, and Egypt. With an interdisciplinary background in natural science and transpersonal psychology/esoteric studies, his doctorate thesis examines the intuition from the perspectives of quantum physics, neurophysiology, psychology, and ancient wisdom's teachings.

As part of his diverse background he has also spent five years in the Swedish Special Forces, shortly worked as a Yoga teacher in Rishikesh, India, and has extensive training in therapeutic modalities such as clinical hypnosis, neurofeedback, and trauma releasing exercises (TRE).

Dr. Nordstrom is also the cocreator of Wabing—a method that uses stretching, self-myofascial release (SMR) and neurogenic tremoring to release tension in the body and achieve a peaceful and relaxed state of mind. www.wabe.me

Jonas Nordstrom, PhD, MSc

Chapter 7   Connection to All Living Things: The Beauty of Relationships

Dr. Butaney is program dean for clinical psychology at the Arizona School of Professional Psychology, where he also serves as core faculty. He is licensed as a psychologist in both Arizona and New York, and maintains a practice in Phoenix and Scottsdale. He earned his doctoral degree from St. John's University, NYC, and a master's degree from Harvard University, Massachusetts.

While in New York City, Dr. Butaney was assistant dean, program director, and faculty at the Derner Institute for Advanced Psychological Studies (Adelphi University). He also served as senior psychologist and director of externship training at Jacobi Medical Center, and worked as senior consulting psychologist at R.G. Psychological Services and the Parker Jewish Institute.

Bhupin Butaney, PhD

Dr. Butaney developed a graduate course in clinical mindfulness and engages in research in the area. He is also very interested in integrating eastern and western perspectives on mindfulness into clinical practice.

Samuel Chates, LMSW, RYT, is an integrative social worker with The James M. Cox Foundation Center for Cancer Prevention and Integrative Oncology at Banner MD Anderson Cancer Center. He is the founder of The Mindfulness Community at Arizona State University; has taught the course, Stress Management Tools, at Arizona State University; has served as a board member for the National Association of Social Workers–Arizona Chapter; and is a Yoga Alliance registered yoga teacher.

Samuel Chates, LMSW, RYT

About *Beyond Stress: Strategies for Blissful Living*

May every day be like a flower
Exciting the senses
At one with nature
Living life to the fullest
In the moment

Maria Napoli

Living in the twenty-first century often drives one to depend upon modern conveniences and technology to save time, do the labor once done by hand or many hands and offers one the opportunity to do more in any given day. There is no argument here regarding the benefits of modern times. Your experience through "Beyond Stress: Strategies for Blissful Living" will offer you the opportunity to tap in to your natural resources that may have gone underground, lost quality and become underutilized as a result of today's fast paced, convenience oriented world. Finding the balance of enjoying the benefits of today's conveniences while keeping our innate and precious gifts necessary for the best quality of life, foods that nourish, tuning into nature, clean air, soil and water, embracing relaxation and listening to our instincts, the source of our truth is the message we want to communicate to you in "Beyond Stress: Strategies for Blissful Living."

As you navigate and explore each chapter we hope you will 1) stimulate your mind and emotions through the research and thoughts the authors share; 2) engage in activities to experience the essence of each chapter; 3) reflect on each chapter by answering questions related to the content and 4) complete a personal journal entry synthesizing what you learned and take away from the chapter through the lens of mindfulness.

As you take in the information of each chapter, begin to deepen your mindfulness by using the four step Mindful MAC Guide. Approach each experience by. . . .

INSTEAD OF . . .

RESPONDING TO YOUR EXPERIENCE. . .

REACTING TO YOUR EXPERIENCE

4 Step MAC Guide

Mindfully
acknowledge
attention
accept
choose

1. Empathically *acknowledging* your experience just as it is without trying to change it. Too often when we are not happy about our experience we may fall into the pit of saying, "If it could have been this way, it should be that way, it did not happen like this last time, why did it happen like this now? I did not expect this." Remember, the best possible arrangement always prevails, whether or not it meets our expectations or desire.

2. Intentionally pay *attention* to your experiences. Notice the many reactions your body may have, tight muscles, sensations, shallow breath, or racing, or ruminating thoughts. Remember, *responding* to your experience instead of *reacting* will help you make the best choice where you are better able to listen to your instincts and not be ruled by your 'mindless monster,' taking you out of the moment.

3. *Accept* your experience without Judgment. We have this moment and this experience one time only. Simply stated, it's a one-stop shop deal. There is a reason why life is not perfect. Lessons, and more lessons to be learned from our experiences help us to grow and change so that we make better choices along our life journey. This may be the most difficult step to master in your mindful practice as "We want what we want" and get stuck all too often in feeling disappointed when our expectations of others and ourselves are not met. You may have been told by your parents that a "dollar earned is more appreciated than being given a dollar." In this respect the same is true without experiences, we may have to work a bit harder when things do not go our way, yet we learn the benefit of the lesson, which goes a long way, maybe for life.

4. *Choose Your Experience.* Although change may cause fear, discomfort, and anxiety, it is a natural process of life. We cannot move forward without change and making a choice to accept our experiences and view them with the 'eyes of child' can be invigorating and exciting. Take a chance on yourself, embrace life, live mindfully.

Before and after reading each chapter, take time to practice your mindful breathing by listening to one of the three 10 minute tracks in the Mindful MAC Breathing site, or even better, listen to all of them. Maria Napoli and Susan Busatti Giangano have created the tracks with beautiful photos and music to set the mood for your mindful practice. By setting the stage for "being in the zone" you will be able to get the most out of your experience.

In chapter one, "Mindful Reflections of Blissful Living," Maria Napoli reviews your Mindful MAC Guide through storytelling. As you read through the rest of the book, keep the Mindful MAC Guide in the forefront as you deepen your ability to be mindful in all of your experiences.

Photograph courtesy of Maria Napoli

In chapter two, "The Joy of Living in the Parasympathetic System," David Berceli takes you on a journey through your nervous system as he guides you to move away from unnecessary fight or flight reactions toward living in a rest and healing state, the parasympathetic nervous system. Allow yourself to imagine the mechanics of what is actually going on when your experience stress and ignite the sympathetic nervous system. Through your mindful presence, you will begin to understand how to respond differently to stress and activate the parasympathetic nervous system, which offers you the gift of rest, recovery, and healing.

Image © Michael Pettigrew, 2014. Used under license from Shutterstock, Inc.

In chapter three, "Whole Person Health Across the Lifespan," Steve Peterson walks you through infancy to older adulthood. With his innovation and humor he narrates how stress impacts life right from the beginning, before we leave the womb, and how we might change that path as adults.

Photograph courtesy of Maria Napoli

In chapter four, "Sustainable Living and Conscious Eating" Lisa Schmidt writes reflectively on how the food industry has changed, and how it has impacted our health. As you read the chapter and practice the activities, you will begin to make decisions to let go of old eating habits, create new options where you buy your foods and choose your foods, but also learn how your food choices travel throughout your body from assimilation to digestion and finally, elimination. Understanding what actually happens in your body when you eat gives you a window to view the process and make decisions for choosing healthy nutrition.

Photograph courtesy of Maria Napoli

In chapter five, "Impact of Global Environmental Stress on Universal Well-Being: Be the Solution," Patricia Duryea discusses how the past has influenced the present in the way we live and the impact of environmental stress upon humans and the planet. Offering you an opportunity to rethink how decreasing your carbon footprint can improve your own life and the lives of our future generation will be discussed.

Photograph courtesy of Maria Napoli

In chapter six, "The Science of Instincts and Intuition," Jonas Nordstrom with his keen scientific mind explains how we, as humans, have the potential to use more of our brainpower than you ever imagined. Put on your 'brain helmet,' you will begin to realize that the information available to you through your instinct and intuition awaits, bringing you to 'outer limits' of knowing and being.

Photograph courtesy of Maria Napoli

In chapter seven, "Connection to All Living Things: The Beauty of Relationships," Bhupin Butaney and Sam Chates poetically discuss the power of our relationships. When we are mindful, we are able to make healthy choices in our relationships. How we show up, with empathy, compassion, and nonjudgment, listening with all of our senses is the cornerstone for happiness. Our connection to significant relations, family, friends, coworkers, people in our everyday interactions in our community and equally important, our connection to nature and all living things will be discussed. This chapter will guide you to reflect upon your past and current relationships and mindfully move you to make decisions to add more joy, love, and mindful compassion every day you encounter others and yourself.

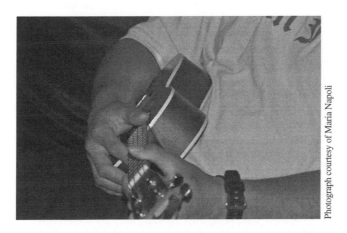

Photograph courtesy of Maria Napoli

In chapter eight, "Happiness is Bliss: Paying it Forward," Maria Napoli brings your experience to an end by reflecting upon how you can bring love and joy out into the world. Keep the expression "You cannot have it until you give it away" in mind as you move forward in your interactions with the environment and people that impact your life.

CHAPTER ONE

MINDFUL REFLECTIONS OF BLISSFUL LIVING
By Maria Napoli

Photograph courtesy of Maria Napoli

My Mind is Empty
My senses are keen
Nurtured in nature
I am filled with love

Maria Napoli

4 Step **MAC** Guide

Mindfully
acknowledge
attention
accept
choose

Mindful Eating: A Piece of the Foot-Long Sub-Hero

Regina was excited to visit her family and particularly looking forward to the delicious food that would be served. She lived in a remote part of the state and did not have the opportunity to eat some of the traditional foods of her culture, yummy Italian delicacies. One of her favorite foods was the Italian sub-hero, which contained imported spices, oils, cheeses, and meat delicacies. She thought about it for weeks before the

Image © R.Ashrafov, 2014. Used under license from Shutterstock, Inc.

gathering. When she arrived at her cousin's home, she immediately saw a long table set up with many foods. Regina walked up to the table and stood still for a moment while observing her favorites.

Taking in the vision with her eyes of the foot-long Italian sub sandwich was a feast for Regina's eyes. The smell of olive oil and garlic along with the sharp Parmesan cheese was intoxicating. Acknowledging that having one piece would be enough, Regina proceeded to take her slice to the table. She paid attention to the acute explosion of her senses. She spent a few moments looking at the crunchy Italian bread covered with sesame seeds. The sandwich was piled high with delicious cheeses, peppers, tomatoes, and meat delicacies. She slowly picked up the sandwich and took the first bite, savoring the taste of each ingredient. Listening to the crunch in her mouth sounded like walking on freshly packed snow. Taking in the aroma, she envisioned the bread being baked in the oven. As she began to slowly chew, activating the digestive enzymes, a variety of tastes began to emerge in her mouth.

To her surprise, a piece of bread got stuck in her tooth while eating. She began to feel distracted and felt annoyed that her experience was disturbed by the occurrence. Going back to her sandwich, Regina decided to ignore the bread sitting in her tooth for the duration of the eating experience and let go of the distraction and annoyance and went back enjoying the delicacy experience. She reflected on how much she savored each bite. Regina's mindfully making a choice to accept her experience without judgment made the Italian sub a hero for the day.

Image © Alan Bailey, 2014. Used under license from Shutterstock, Inc.

Growing Young with Age: Dancing the Night Away

Charlie was celebrating his 95th birthday. He did not feel his age; in fact, he was more active than most members of his family. He loved gardening, writing, and visiting with friends, and his favorite past time was ballroom dancing. He heard that the local dance studio was having a contest, and

Charlie was excited about participating with his wife of fifty years, Clara. The challenge and passion were the ingredients that drove their motivation to compete. Charlie invited his children and grandchildren to come to the event. The family in general was not happy about Charlie and Clara's decision to dance. They felt that they might have a heart attack and were being overzealous. Charlie acknowledged the fact that his family worried about him. Although he did have a heart attack two decades ago, his health was actually quite good since he was more active and dancing several times a week. Without looking back and staying in the moment, Charlie simply acknowledged his family's concern. He paid attention, nevertheless, to his disappointment in his family's assumptions and negative perspective. He also was aware of some tension in his gut as he was holding onto feelings that were not expressed. When Charlie accepted his experience regarding his family's reaction to his decision to compete in the contest, he was able to make a choice to sit down and respond to his family's concern. Once they talked things out and Charlie reminded them that he and Clara have been dancing regularly, the family felt more positive. They also acknowledged that they have been busy with their own lives and were not aware of the activities Charlie and Clara have been involved in. Charlie enjoyed his birthday celebration doing what he loved to do with his sweetheart, and sharing the event with his family made all the difference.

Intuitive Smartness: Listening to the Gut

Justin has been a successful student finding his academic studies an enjoyable experience as he was diligent, stayed on task, and had good study habits. He felt that learning was an opportunity to see the world from many perspectives. The one area of Justin's life where he had difficulty was meeting new people. He saw himself as a shy person who battled with negative self-talk. Controlling his mindless monster, "Judgmental Justin," presented a challenge, particularly when he was interested in a girl he wanted to date. He found that he isolated himself and was too often overly immersed in his studies fearing rejection upon meeting new people. His friend Luigi invited him to a small dinner party. He invited a young woman whom he thought would be a match for Justin. Although Justin wanted to attend, he was equally anxious about the event. He spent some time imagining the situation and how he would behave, what conversation would transpire, would he get food stuck in his teeth and become embarrassed, and so on, with a controlling mindless monster, "Judgmental Justin," dominating his experience.

Justin decided that he would try mindful meditation and practiced for two weeks before the dinner. He became acutely aware that he made assumptions and negatively predicted outcomes of situations before they occurred. He practiced listening to his instincts, staying in the moment, and embracing his experiences during his daily activities.

The day finally came when Justin was to attend the dinner at Luigi's home. Luigi shared some information about Elizabeth, the young woman who would be there. He liked everything he heard about

Elizabeth. Justin arrived early and anticipated the introduction. When Elizabeth finally arrived, Justin immediately felt a connection to her, their eyes met with a gleam. Soon his "mindless monster" began negative self-talk—thoughts that Elizabeth might not like him, what would he say to her if they were alone, and on and on. Justin acknowledged that his "mindless monster" was trying to control the situation, yet he also acknowledged that his instincts communicated a very positive connection with Elizabeth. He paid attention to the thoughts he was having, yet did not let them control the situation. He accepted his experience, his mindless monster "Judgmental Justin" as well as the warm connection he felt toward Elizabeth without judgment. Justin made a choice to thoroughly enjoy the dinner and conversation that took place that evening. To his surprise, Elizabeth invited him to a play the following week. Needless to say, Justin's instinct that she liked him was accurate; he quieted his "mindless monster" and looked forward to getting to know Elizabeth.

The Ecstasy of the Stretch: Bring on the Parasympathetic System

Tasha remembers the accident as if it happened yesterday. She was on her way to a movie to meet a friend when a van driver passed a red light and hit her car. Although the injuries she incurred were not fatal, she nevertheless, spent a year recovering from broken bones in both her legs and arms. Each time she got behind the wheel, the memories of the accident created fear.

Image © Stephen Orsillo, 2014. Used under license from Shutterstock, Inc.

Being in the state of fight or flight became a familiar occurrence. Tasha wanted to find a way to relax and let go, but was unable to find a way to do so. Although her injuries were healed, Tasha still experienced her body as damaged. She resisted riding her bike, an activity she previously enjoyed, for fear of falling or getting hit by a car. Her best friend Kinisha had been taking yoga classes and told Tasha stories about her experiences of feeling relaxed and limber. Tasha wished that she could have a similar experience and move out of her place of fear that plagued her and prevented her from trying new things. One day she was invited to observe the yoga class with Kinisha. As she watched the students practice breathing techniques and move in and out of the stretches, her negative self-talk reminded her of the accident and taking a risk to try the stretches might injure her limbs in some way. Tasha was conflicted. One the one hand, she wanted to participate in the class and, at best, experience relaxation. On the other hand, she feared becoming injured. After going back and forth for several weeks thinking about the class, she finally made a decision to engage.

As Tasha placed her mat on the floor, she settled in with trepidation. The instructor began guiding a breathing exercise. Tasha noticed her shallow breath and began to judge herself. Her "mindless monster," "Fearful Tasha," was gearing up to squash a positive experience. Following the breathing exercise, the instructor guided the class into a gentle forward bend stretch. Tasha immediately felt limber as her muscles relaxed and stretched. Her breathing became deeper furthering the relaxation experience. As her "mindless monster," "Fearful Tasha," began to creep in with negative self-talk, Tasha acknowledge the pleasure she was experiencing. She focused on how warm and limber her muscles felt and let go of thinking what could happen. She paid attention to her initial anxiety, but also noticed that her sense of hearing was keener listening to the nurturing tone and pace of the yoga instructor furthering relaxation. Tasha also acknowledged that her monkey mind still tried to control her experience.

Throughout the class, Tasha accepted the thoughts, feelings, and body awareness without judgment. She consciously made a choice to enjoy the flow of the stretches, welcoming the limber and energizing sensations. Tasha made a commitment to come back for another class. Letting go of fear, which kept her locked into the sympathetic nervous system of fight or flight, and moving into the parasympathetic nervous system of rest and healing is a decision that now dominated her desire and goal.

Man and Nature: The Beauty of Relationships

Randy worked as an accountant for most of his life. At forty-five, he pondered about his life and began feeling resentful that he had little to show for his efforts at the large accounting firm he had labored in for decades. After many broken promises for a big promotion, Randy was tired of witnessing his boss' continued "high-class" lifestyle while he labored to support his wife and two children to make ends meet. His boss took several vacations and long lunches and often took credit for the work Randy completed with the "big clients." Since Randy was not an assertive man and he did make many attempts to follow up on the promise for a promotion, he decided to take matters into his own hands. One day, Randy was working on the company's financial statements. He began to embezzle small amounts of money, which escalated to larger amounts. His boss did not notice the loss until he realized that over half a million dollars was unaccounted for. Enraged with the discovery that Randy stole the money, the authorities were called and Randy was sentenced to ten years in prison.

Image © wichan kijchanpaiboon, 2014. Used under license from Shutterstock, Inc.

Randy wondered what possessed him to commit such a crime, yet he had plenty of time to sort out what was truly important in life. Needless to say, prison offered no luxuries or pleasantries, yet there was an opportunity to engage in developing a garden. Randy took great pride and developed a new perspective for gratitude and a connection to life. The ugliness of prison took on a new meaning as he felt the connection to the flowers and plants that were growing in the garden. Every day Randy empathically acknowledges the joy he felt being a part of the growing process of life. He did not complain about what he did not have or want, but embraced the experience. He intentionally paid attention every day to his finely tuned senses that were developing as he worked closely to the earth and emotions of gratitude for the connection to the beauty of nature. Although at times he felt resentful that his boss was still living the "swanky" life while he was imprisoned, he did not judge either himself for having those feelings or his boss for the lifestyle. Randy made the choice to enjoy each moment and began making plans for how he would change his attitude and life when he was released. In fact, he had received the news that he would be paroled after serving only five years for good behavior and taking initiative to work with his fellow prison-mates developing the garden which everyone benefited from. Randy learned a lifelong lesson that one can receive great joy from the simplest experiences.

4 Step **MAC** Guide

Mindfully

acknowledge
attention
accept
choose

At One with the Outdoors: Being in the Zone

Valentina lived an active life. She cherished the four children she was raising, yet found time for herself to exercise. She loved nature, and hiking in the desert was where she found peace of mind. This was her time to let go of all responsibilities and "just be." Although she had a large family and often hiked with a cousin or sister, she mostly enjoyed hiking by herself. This was her time, her meditation and connection with nature. On one unfortunate day, Valentina tripped over a boulder and shattered her hip. As she was being transported to the hospital, all she could think of was that her hiking days were over. Valentina acknowledged that her days of hiking would change. She paid attention to her feelings of disappointment and a sensation of feeling "blue." She had negative thoughts that her exercise routine would be limited to the house. Valentina also judged herself for not being more careful while she was hiking, thinking that the fall could have been prevented.

She recovered well from hip replacement surgery with months of physical therapy and support from her family. During this time, she began exercising in her pool with her physical therapist. To her surprise, she found that being immersed in the water offered her a similar experience to hiking, solitude, quiet, and relaxation while having a nice workout. Valentina acknowledged that although she would not hike as rigorously as before, she found a new love, swimming. She paid attention to new sensations experienced while in the pool, such as feeling nurtured and warmth, and enjoyed the sunshine bathing her while she swam. She accepted her new experience with joy and realized that she had a choice to swim as often as she wished and could still hike given her limitations. With the help of her family, solar panels were installed on the house, giving Valentina more time to swim during the year. With the freshness of a child, and seeing her experiences from a new perspecitve, she did not lose her time hiking, and not only did she gain another opportunity to heal her body, but she was also able to quiet her thoughts and mindfully enjoy her life.

MINDFUL AWARENESS REFLECTION JOURNAL

Choose one mindful experience as you begin your reflection.

Empathically Acknowledge

Describe your experience

_____

_____

_____

Intentional Attention

Describe what you noticed

Breath	
Body	
Emotions	
Thoughts	
Senses	

Accept Without Judgment

Describe judgment; acceptance

_____

_____

_____

Willingly Choose

Intention/willingness; new perspective

_____

_____

_____

Mindful Mac Meditation

Describe your meditation experiences. What did you learn?

_____

_____

_____

CHAPTER TWO

THE JOY OF LIVING IN THE PARASYMPATHETIC SYSTEM

By David Berceli

Photograph courtesy of Maria Napoli

Breathe
Rest
Think positive thoughts
I am healing

Maria Napoli

Emotions such as stress, anxiety, tension, and fear are all part of common human existence; however, your life experiences also contain emotions and experiences such as love, comfort, relaxation, safety, and pleasure. Although you may not like the stressful experiences and prefer the relaxing ones, you have an amazing nervous system that helps you to deal with all these experiences in a very successful and balanced manner. In this chapter, you will look at how your nervous system not only helps you deal with these diverse situations in life but also interact with and help your nervous system to grow, learn, and adapt to all of life's situations in a healthy manner.

Divisions of the Nervous System

In order to understand how to help control the responses and reactions of your nervous system you need to understand how the nervous system is designed. Although the nervous system is very complex, its design is somewhat simple to understand. If you understand its design, you can work very easily with your nervous system to help you maintain a balance of healthy stress and relaxation.

There are two main parts of the human nervous system, the central nervous system (CNS) and the peripheral nervous system (PNS). The CNS contains the brain and the spinal cord. The PNS can be divided into two parts, the voluntary nervous system and the involuntary nervous system (also known as the autonomic nervous system). Since you have voluntary control and involuntary control capabilities built into your nervous system, you are able to work with and help your nervous system regulate between states of stress and relaxation.

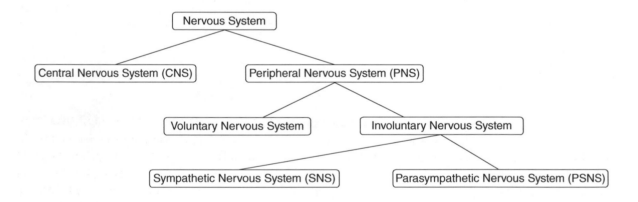

The sympathetic nervous system (SNS) is the part of the nervous system that speeds us up or stimulates you to be alert for your fight-or-flight response in case you encounter unexpected danger or threat. The parasympathetic nervous system (PSNS) is in charge of calming you down and putting you into a state referred to as rest and digest. Both of these systems are generally operating unconsciously in us throughout the day. They are meant to be complimentary to each other so that you have both the amount of energy and relaxation you need each day to live in a balanced and healthy manner.

It is obvious that the types of fast-paced, active lives we generally find in our culture often keep our SNS activated more often. Unfortunately, you stimulate the SNS when there is no

danger, for example, being stuck in traffic, charging up when someone cuts in front of you in line or firing up when your expectations are not met. The overactivation of your SNS causes a strain on your body and also inhibits your ability to activate your PSNS to calm you down at the end of the day. However, when you do sport activities or some type of mindfulness or relaxation activity, you are able to take conscious control of your involuntary nervous system. It is this ability to take conscious control of an involuntary system that allows you to self-regulate your nervous system responses to various situations you experience throughout the day. In short, it is this conscious control of an involuntary nervous system

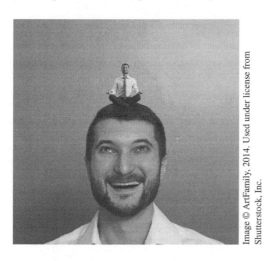

Image © ArtFamily, 2014. Used under license from Shutterstock, Inc.

that allows you to determine your emotional state of anger or calmness, fear or safety, happiness or sadness.

The SNS is working all the time. This means that your nervous system is constantly turned on and it is always in its alert or energetic mode to help provide you with daily energy and protect you from any danger that may unexpectedly occur to you. Therefore, the SNS is only slowed downed when the PSNS interrupts it. So you need to deliberately activate your PSNS to provide the input that inhibits or turns off the SNS.[1]

Now that you understand how the nervous system works, you want to look at the relationship between the nervous system and the brain and the body. Let's look at the brain and the body by dissecting them into different parts to help us understand how specific parts of the brain and the body deliberately communicate with each other to keep us healthy. Let's first look at the brain and the different parts that help us both activate for protection and deactivate for relaxation.

The Brain and the Nervous System

You are going to look at the brain in three simple parts, the brainstem, the limbic system or midbrain, and the cortex. These three parts of the brain help you understand in a simple manner how the brain activates during stress and deactivates when it feels safe. The brainstem is one of the most primitive parts of the brain that activates unconsciously. It helps to control and regulate basic life-giving mechanisms such as your heart rate, blood pressure, and respiration or breathing. The limbic system or midbrain is another primitive part of the brain that helps to control basic human emotions such as your fight-or-flight response when you are feeling threatened. The cortex or neocortex is the newest part of our brain, and this is considered the part of the human brain that allows us to reflect on and to think about ourselves in a way that separates us from other species. In order to ensure that you are protected at all times, the brainstem and limbic system are activated by the autonomic nervous system that keeps you on alert for any potential danger. Here is an example of how these three parts of the brain function together. When you perceive something as a real or imagined threat, the brainstem automatically elevates your heart rate, blood pressure, and breathing. It does this in preparation for a possible fight-or-flight response that you might need to have to survive this perceived or real threat. As soon as the brainstem activates itself, the limbic system immediately becomes involved because it will create an emotion to accompany the activation of the brain stem. When these activate together, you now have a rapid heart rate to pump the blood to the extremities in order to run or fight the threat and you also have an emotion to give us the excited charge that you need to survive the threat. With the activation of these two parts of the brain, you now

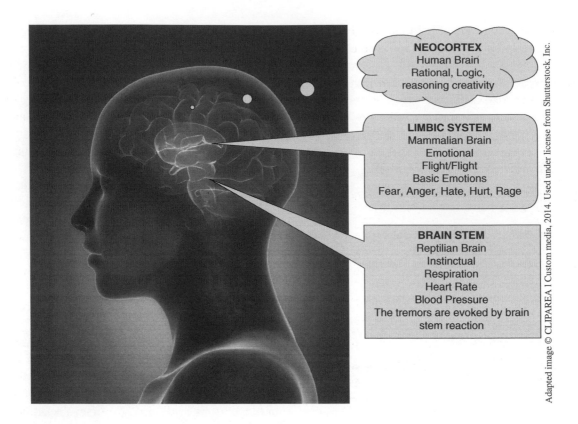

NEOCORTEX
Human Brain
Rational, Logic,
reasoning creativity

LIMBIC SYSTEM
Mammalian Brain
Emotional
Flight/Flight
Basic Emotions
Fear, Anger, Hate, Hurt, Rage

BRAIN STEM
Reptilian Brain
Instinctual
Respiration
Heart Rate
Blood Pressure
The tremors are evoked by brain
stem reaction

Adapted image © CLIPAREA I Custom media, 2014. Used under license from Shutterstock, Inc.

have an excited heart rate, high blood pressure, and rapid breathing along with the emotions such as fear, anger, rage, and so on to help you survive this threat.

Once these two parts of the brain have activated, they then begin to have a strong effect on the way you can use the cortex or the logical, rational part of our brain. If they remain activated long enough, they will produce impulsive, shortsighted, or even violent behavior, and increased stress-related diseases. This is why when you are under stress, you have difficulty concentrating, memorizing, remembering, or acting rationally. Since the brainstem and limbic system are more primitive parts of the brain and they have control over the logical part of the brain, you find yourself at the mercy of your autonomic nervous system. In the brain, that autonomic nervous system is located in the brainstem; however, it then extends into the PNS that goes throughout the entire body. These two parts of the brain actually have more control over our conscious part of the brain. This is why you can sometimes experience fear or anger even at times when you do not want to have those emotions.

Image © Fabio Berti, 2014. Used under license from Shutterstock, Inc.

You can often find yourself trying to convince yourself by using the cortex that you need to stay calm, you need to breathe slowly, and you need to think rationally—and even when you try to do this, at times you cannot control the brain and the body to be able to respond to your wishes. An example is when a friend says something that irritates you but you don't want to get angry; however, you can't stop the surge of emotional energy that seems to erupt out of you even when you decided that you wanted to stay calm and talk about the situation. If these more primitive parts of the brain continue to control your cortex over a long period of time, this is what leads to impulsive, shortsighted, or even violent behavior. This is also what leads to increased anxiety, depression, substance abuse, learning disorders, and increased stress-related diseases.[2]

When the brainstem and limbic system activate, they change the entire communication system in the body. As the blood vessels constrict and the blood is pushed into the extremities, the body begins to contract and activate with adrenaline and cortisol to insure that you can move the body fast enough or your body is protected strong enough to survive the threat—this means that the muscles become tight, the fascia constricts, and the body engages itself in a manner that causes the sensation of tension in the body—this is precisely why you experience physical sensations such as back pains, gastrointestinal problems, and fatigue when you are under stress. The body is actually being manipulated by the brain and the nervous system in an unconscious manner that produces these new physical sensations of discomfort in the body. If you do not turn off these parts of the brain and send new signals through the nervous system, you develop what you call chronic symptoms of pain or stress-related diseases. Simple examples of this are when you are hunched over a desk for hours, at a certain point the body will signal you to stretch backward on the chair or stand up, take a walk, and so forth. If you ignore these signals because you have to cram for an exam, you will often find yourself unable to sleep, feel fatigued, have back ache or neck ache, and so on.

This protective mechanism of the primitive parts of the brain along with the autonomic nervous system are the perfect design to ensure that you can stay on alert for any possible danger and survive it. Unfortunately, it is also this communication of the brain and nervous system that cause you not to be able to calm yourself down as quickly as you would like. At the end of this chapter, you will look at some practices that enable you to be able to calm down the brainstem and limbic system so that you can gain access to the cortex and therefore your logical and rational thinking after you have experienced a traumatic or stressful event. It is only after you are capable of becoming activated for the fight-or-flight response and then deactivated after the threat is over that you are truly capable of living as resilient and healthy human being.

The Human Body and the Nervous System Communication

Image © Fabio Berti, 2014. Used under license from Shutterstock, Inc.

One way to create change in your nervous system is to use your body. Since the brain and the body are one integrated system, you can use your thoughts to control your body or you can use your body to control your thoughts. Considerable research has been done on how simple exercise can affect the nervous system. You can pump up the nervous system through rapid strenuous exercises such as running, boxing, swimming, or competition sports or you can calm down the nervous system by using more relaxing techniques such as yoga, Tai Chi, Qigong, or tension and trauma releasing exercises (TRE).[3] Likewise, research has also demonstrated that cognitive practices such as meditation or mindfulness can have a profound impact on quieting the nervous system. There are changes in certain parts of the brain, as you just saw, that cause accompanying adaptive changes in the body, and this is done through the autonomic nervous system.[4] Likewise, by stimulating nerve fibers in the skin, muscle, and fascia, you are able to deliberately provide corrective feedback to the brain to help it to activate a parasympathetic response.

Just as you look at the different parts of the brain to understand how they work together and independently, let's look at different parts of the body and how they work together both independently and separately.

Fascia/Body and Nervous System

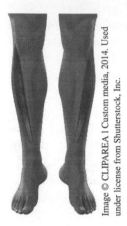

Image © CLIPAREA 1 Custom media, 2014. Used under license from Shutterstock, Inc.

One of the most wonderful things about your nervous system is that it is directly connected to the myofascia of the human body. *Myofascia* is the inseparable nature of muscle tissue (Myo-) and its accompanying connective tissue (fascia).[5] A simple explanation is that fascia is like a plastic bag that surrounds muscles but it is then interconnected with all ligaments, tendons, bone, and muscle inside the body. Actually, your nervous system receives its greatest amount of sensory input from your myofascial tissues.[6]—this means that your body can be manipulated or deliberately used in ways that help to control your nervous system. It is this bidirectional communication between the myofascia of the body and the nervous system that allows you to be able to successfully use physical practices to help control and regulate your nervous system.

Now that you understand you can use the body to help calm down the brain, let's look more specifically at how you can do this. Just as you need to understand how the nervous system is designed in order to have a positive effect on your body, you also have to understand how the body is designed so that you can use it to have a positive effect on the nervous system.

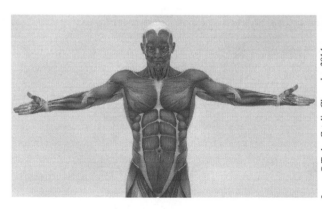

Image © Tudor Catalin Gheorghe, 2014. Used under license from Shutterstock, Inc.

First of all, let's look at something simple like the muscles in the body. The anterior muscles in the front of the body (which include the obliquus externus abdominis, the obliquus internus abdominis, and the rectus abdominus) are primarily activated by the SNS. Therefore when the SNS activates, the flexor muscles in the front of the body are activated and this causes the extensor muscles in the back of the body to be inhibited.[1(p. 81)]

Image © CLIPAREA 1 Custom media, 2014. Used under license from Shutterstock, Inc.

The opposite is also true. The posterior muscles (which are muscles that run throughout the posterior side of the body such as the gluteus maximus, erector spinae muscle group, trapezius, and posterior deltoids) are primarily activated by the PSNS. Therefore, when the PSNS activates the spinal extensor muscles (erector spinae, semispinalis, and multifidi, which are layered muscles running throughout the length of the posterior spine) in the back of the body, this allows us to come into softer, relaxed, and more upright posture.

With this simple understanding of the front and the back of the body, you can see how sitting at a desk or curling the body forward contracts the muscles in the front of the body and automatically stimulates the SNS. Without realizing it as you work on your computers, sit at your desk, or read books in the library in a sitting position, you're constantly stimulating the SNS. It is a common experience that after you have been sitting for a while you naturally start to stretch the body backward arching the back by leaning over the back of the chair as a way of pulling the muscles in the front of the body into a big stretch so you can relax them. This is a simple example of how your body sends you a signal to start stretching the front muscles of the body so they can begin to release allowing the back muscles to activate and bring you into a more relaxed state of parasympathetic response. Another simple example is when you lay down on your back on the bed as a way of activating the muscles in the back of the body and deactivating the muscles in the front of the body. This position actually helps you to fall asleep.

Breathing and the Body–Mind Connection

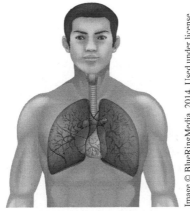

Image © BlueRingMedia, 2014. Used under license from Shutterstock, Inc.

Now you can consider something just as easy to understand, which is the breathing process of the human body. Let's first look at the diaphragm muscle. The diaphragm muscle located at the bottom of the rib cage is a large muscle that controls 75% of our breathing process. It has been long accepted through extensive research that by controlling the breath in the human body you can also help regulate our thoughts, blood pressure, and heart rate.

The movements of the chest during breathing.

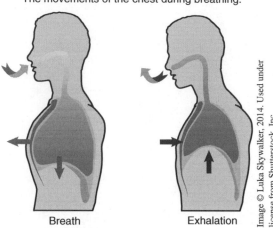

Breath   Exhalation

Image © Luka Skywalker, 2014. Used under license from Shutterstock, Inc.

Shake It Off with the PSNS

You have an amazing mechanism built into your nervous system that helps you automatically calm down after a stressful or traumatic event. Although it is well known and accepted that people tremor or shake out of nervousness before, during, or after stressful events, little research has been done about this shaking response. The technique of TRE mentioned in this chapter activates this shaking mechanism to help activate the PSNS.[7] Medical science has generally studied body shaking and tremors as a pathological expression of the nervous system. As a result of this interpretation of body tremors, little research has been done about the potential therapeutic value of body shaking. In order to understand this shaking mechanism, you have to identify what it is and review the research that has been done to demonstrate how it works.

Body tremors are defined as the rhythmic, involuntary oscillatory movement of a body part.[8] These tremors have basically been studied in three fields of medical science, namely, psychology, neurology, and physiology. The science of psychology basically classifies body tremors under two categories, rest tremors and postural tremors.[9] These tremors are often referred to as psychogenic tremors or posttraumatic tremors. The *DSM5* uses these tremors as diagnostic features for panic attacks, social phobia, generalized anxiety disorder, and posttraumatic stress disorder.[10] Through this analysis, the tremors are seen as a pathological expression of the body during times of stress.

Image © cherezoff, 2014. Used under license from Shutterstock, Inc.

The science of neurology has also done considerable research on body tremors.[11] The science of neurology has basically studied body tremors as a result of neurological diseases such as Parkinson's disease, cerebellar lesions, muscular dystrophy, and the like. They have also studied the body tremors as psychogenic tremors that are the result of somatization of past history. Once again the field of neurology has studied the tremors as a disturbance or a reaction in the human body that is a direct response to a disturbing past event.

The field of physiology is the only science that has studied body tremors with potential therapeutic benefit. Body tremors in the field of physiology were first studied in the 1960s as rhythmic neuromuscular stimulation (RNS).[12] By mechanically stimulating a shaking or tremoring response in the human body, it was recognized that tremors are helpful in physiological rehabilitation. Mechanical stimulation of muscular tremors later developed into fields of rehabilitation known as vibrational therapy, biomechanical stimulation, and whole body vibration.[13] It was recognized that muscular vibration helped the coordination of the musculoskeletal and nervous system; it provided pain relief, increased muscle strength, and improved range of motion. The TRE routine has consistently demonstrated many of the same physiological responses as mentioned above. However, they also have the added benefit of reducing stress, tension, and anxiety that can often be the result of stressful or traumatic events.[14] By activating this tremor mechanism voluntarily in a safe environment, the body tremors have the opportunity to com-

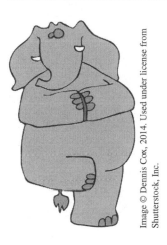

Image © Dennis Cox, 2014. Used under license from Shutterstock, Inc.

plete the discharge that was aborted at the time of the traumatic or stressful event. By completing this natural relaxation response of the PSNS, the body is finally able to return it back to a calm and restful state. This technique is part of the autonomic nervous system and therefore does not require cognitive processing to achieve a successful completion of stress reduction. In brief, by using this technique you can reduce your stress, tension, and anxiety without much cognitive effort. You can, as is stated in the title of this chapter, enjoy living in the PSNS by using its own activation to restore you back to a peaceful, relaxed, and calm state.

As noted earlier, you can calm down the nervous system by using more relaxing techniques such as yoga, Tai Chi, Quigong, or TRE.[15] Likewise, research has also demonstrated that cognitive practices such as meditation or mindfulness can have a profound impact on quieting the nervous system.

Yoga

Yoga has been studied since the 1960s by various medical organizations and institutions. Although there are many types of yoga, all of them typically combine physical postures, breathing techniques, and meditation or relaxation. The results following a pose can be a revived sense of energy and/or relaxation. Both experiences stimulate the PSNS. A comprehensive review of yoga research can be found online at the National Center for Complimentary and Alternative Medicine (NCCAM), which is a branch of the National Institute of Health (NIH).[16] The reported benefits of yoga range from improvement of physical flexibility[17] to psycho-emotional stability.[18]

Practice 1

At the risk of oversimplifying the beauty and complexity of intense yoga practices, there are a few simple yoga practices you can do without much training. Simply standing on one leg for an extended period of time will force your mind to concentrate on the present moment, activate specific signals from the muscles for you to maintain balance, and cause your breathing to slow down. This simple technique has the ability to alter breathing, stimulate body awareness, and reduce the mind's distractions to focus on the present moment.

Image © vita khorzhevska, 2014. Used under license from Shutterstock, Inc.

Practice 2

A simple stretching of the spine can interrupt the normal tension pattern you hold in your spine as a result of common repetitive movements. Take a pillow or blanket roll, lay it on the floor, and lie over it on your back. This exercise will extend the spine as a way of complimenting the normal posture of flexion or leaning forward, which you often do in daily life. In this position, the diaphragm will begin to stretch passively and the body will begin to breathe more deeply thereby activating the PSNS.

Practice 3

The yoga practice of psycho-emotional stability boils down to being in the present moment. Fear and anxiety are almost always a result of something that has happened or something that you anticipate will happen. Living in the present moment reduces all the brain's signals to our simple surroundings. There are many simple ways to focus the mind on the present moment. Counting the breath is a very common one. Count how many breaths you take in one minute. Then when you have the number, try to decrease the number of breaths you take by three in the next minute. This will bring your consciousness to the present moment as well as deliberately cause you to slow down your breathing.

Qigong

Qigong (pronounced chee-gung) is another practice that recognizes the necessity of combining focused concentration with simple movements and balanced breathing in a controlled manner. QiGong is sometimes referred to as *Chinese yoga*. It is an ancient Chinese practice that is used to remove blockages of the body's *life-force energy*. Along with movement exercises, it also includes standing and sitting meditations and energy-building practices. The concept of qigong is that body tightness and stiff muscles cause a block in natural energetic flow of the body's system. If one practices specific physical exercises, concentration, and energy-generating movements, the body's energy (chi) can be unblocked, which will cause an improvement in one's health. The health benefits include improved brain function, blood flow, and heart function.[19]

Practice 1

The simplest qigong exercise is to stand with your feet shoulder width apart pointing straight forward. This position house your body to feel securely anchored to the ground. Begin the exercise by taking a deep breath in while simultaneously raising your arms from your sides up over top of your head while you inhale. By raising your arms during the inhalation you help to stretch the chest cavity and diaphragm allowing deep breath to occur—now exhale and lower your arms directly in front of you until they are resting again at your side. By exhaling while simultaneously lowering your arms, you bring the body back into a comfortable standing position allowing the breath to completely release from the body. Continue repeating this same movement ten times with a very slow inhalation and exhalation. Once again you can see that slow breathing, concentrating on the present moment, and moving the body are all significant components to activate a PSNS in order to produce the sensation of relaxation and calmness in the body.

Practice 2

Another qigong exercise is to stand with your feet shoulder width apart and your hands at your side. Raise your arms directly in front of you with your hands hanging lamp at the wrist while you inhale. When your arms are directly in front of you, slowly lower them in front of the body while slightly bending your knees. The image of the movement is as though you have two paintbrushes in your hands and you are slowly painting the wall directly in front of you. When you raise your arms your knees straighten, and when you lower your arms your knees bend. The combination of bending and straightening the knees in relationship to raising and lowering the arms invites the entire body into a gentle, flowing, rhythmic movement.

Practice 3

This third exercise is very similar to the other two. Stand with your feet shoulder width apart pointing straight forward. This time your arms are extended in front of you with the palms of your hands pointing together. Now inhale and stretch your arms out as wide as you can. When you exhale bring your arms back together and slowly bend the knees. Continue to repeat this movement in a slow rhythmic manner. Doing this movement ten times will help to stretch and relax the trunk of the body.

Tai Chi

Tai chi is another slow meditative physical exercise designed for relaxation and balance and health. It has a history of being a practice of self-defense. However, this particular concept of self-defense is based on lightness, agility, and softness. Tai chi is a practice of integrated body movement. The movement begins in the feet, it is released through the legs, the motion occurs at the waist, and finally the full expression is experienced by the fingers. The reported medical benefits are pain reduction, improved balance, improved aerobic capacity, reduction in high blood pressure, stress reduction, improved sleep, and increased body strength.[20]

Image © Igor Zakowski, 2014. Used under license from Shutterstock, Inc.

Practice 1

Stand with your feet shoulder width apart and feet pointing straight forward. Turn your hands with your palms upward and begin to inhale as you slowly lift your hands along the centerline of your body. When your hands reach the middle of your chest rotate your palms away from you and continue raising your arms until they are completely stretched above you, and your palms are now pointing upward and your head is tilted slightly backward so that you are looking between your fingers. Now, slowly exhale and lower your outstretched arms down the sides of your body, and your palms are once again pointing toward each other. Repeat this movement ten times.

Practice 2

Inhale and raise the palms of your hands up along the centerline of your body. When your hands reach the middle of your chest, they change in opposite directions. Your right palm points upward while you extend your arm as far as you can, and your left palm points downward as you extend that arm as far as you can. Fully extend your arms in both directions—now return your arms back down to the chest position and invert the position of each palm. Your right palm points downward while you extend your arm as far as you can, and your left palm points upward as you extend that arm as far as you can. Again, fully extend your arms in both directions. Your exhalation occurs when the arms are in their fully extended position, and your inhalation occurs when you bring your arms back down toward the center of the chest.

Image © Javier Brosch, 2014. Used under license from Shutterstock, Inc.

Practice 3

This next tai chi exercise is for rotating the spinal column. As always, stand with your feet shoulder width apart, point your feet straight forward, and keep a soft bend in the knees. In the starting position, take a deep breath and then slowly twist from your hips, rotating your body while you exhale. Your shoulders and your neck should follow the hip rotation so that you have a full spinal twist from the waist to the top of the neck. Begin to inhale as you twist your hips back to the forward position and then slowly continue to rotate them to the opposite side while you exhale. Repeat this process ten times.

Mindful Meditation

Image © Nina Buday, 2014. Used under license from Shutterstock, Inc.

Mindful meditation or mindfulness is different from other forms of meditation. The difference is that mindfulness is not trying to teach us to be in different state. It is the opposite. It is trying to help us to simply be aware of the state that you are already in. It is about being in the present moment unconditionally. This means you observe the state that you are in, no matter what is happening to you, without judging the state—you simply observe it. It is in the observation of this state that you become more aware of and capable of accepting the present moment.[21]

Mindfulness meditation is different from the other practices you just covered. TRE yoga, qigong, and tai chi are primarily body-centered practices used to help calm down the activity of the brain. Mindfulness is using the brain to calm itself down and to bring relaxation to the body. This is a perfect example of how the human body is connected neurologically and physiologically. In body-centered practices, you can use the PNS to bring calmness to brain activity, and in mindful meditation you can use the brain to calm itself down and bring relaxation to the body. This is the healthy dialogue between the two primitive parts of the brain (brainstem and limbic system) and the cortex which is the more logical and rational part of the brain.[22]

4 Step MAC Guide
Mindfully
acknowledge
attention
accept
choose

Practice 1

The primary focus in mindfulness is being aware of what is happening at the present moment. One of the easiest ways to focus your awareness is to become aware of your breath. Since the body is breathing all the time, it acts as a built-in metronome or clock that continues to click. Because of this wonderful body process, you can access your awareness of your breath quite readily. Sit in a relaxed and comfortable position so that the spine is upright and not folded forward. You can also lie for this breathing practice. First you want to acknowledge your breath. Once you are aware of your breath, pay attention to it and observe how you are breathing. After you have observed how your body is breathing, accept this breath without any type of judgment; just be the observer. As you continue to observe your breath, you can gently begin the process of making a choice to bring the maximum amount of oxygen into your body by using your breath.

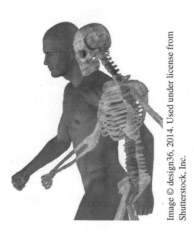

Image © design36, 2014. Used under license from Shutterstock, Inc.

Practice 2

The next important component of mindfulness is the body scan. Sit in a comfortable but alert position with your spine straight up because this exercise can be very calming and could cause sleepiness. As always, it is important to begin a mindful practice with several deep breaths. Scanning the body is the process of observing your body section by section

Image © leedsn, 2014. Used under license from Shutterstock, Inc.

and observing how much sensation you experience in each part of your body. As an example, place your attention on your feet and notice if you have any tension or any specific sensation or have a lack of sensation. Imagine that you can bring your breath into your feet to allow any type of discomfort to begin to release itself. After you have completed bringing your attention to your feet, you can then move your attention into the bottom part of the leg. Notice your calf muscles and notice if there is any particular sensation or lack of sensation. Imagine bringing your breath into your calf muscles to relieve any discomfort you might have in those muscles. Continue to repeat this process of scanning one section of your body at a time bringing your attention and awareness to it and beginning to release any type of tension or discomfort you might have in that section of the body. Repeat this process until you have been able to scan your entire body.

As integrated human beings, the healthiest state is always when there is a balance between the brain and the body.[23] At moments, it is easier to quiet the brain by using body techniques, and at other moments it is easier to relax the body by using cognitive techniques of the brain. The beauty of the human organism is that it is already designed to be an integrated communication between brain and body. You are simply born as an integrated living organism. It is life's difficulties and challenges that can cause a distortion and lack of healthy communication between this brain–body continuum. The most important thought to keep in mind is that your organism is always trying to return to its healthiest state no matter what situation or circumstance may have disturbed it. In this sense, any time you are disturbed you have access to either innate brain-directed interventions or inherent body-directed interventions that are ultimately designed to restore you back to a healthy and calm state. If you can maintain some of the simple practices mentioned in this chapter, you can live more consistently in a healthy, calm, and relaxed state of your parasympathetic nervous system.

References

1. Sumner, G., & Haines, S., *Cranial Intelligence: A Practical Guide to Biodynamic Craniosacral Therapy.* London: Singing Dragon, 2010.

2. Sapolsky, R., *Why Zebras Don't Have Ulcers.* New York: Henry Holt, 2004.

3. Berceli, D., *Trauma Releasing Exercises: A Revolutionary New Method for Stress/trauma Recovery.* Charleston, SC: Create Space, 2005.

4. Taylor, A. G., Goehler, L. E., Galper, D. I., Innes, K. E. & Bourguignon, C. "Top-down and Bottom-up Mechanisms in Mind–body Medicine: Development of an Integrative Framework for Psychophysiological Research," *Explore* 6 no. (1) (2010): 29–41.

5. Myers, T., *Anatomy Trains.* New York: Churchill Livingstone Elsevier, 2010, 4.

6. Schleip, R., "Fascial Plasticity—A New Neurobiological Explanation," Part 1. *Journal of Movement and Bodywork Therapies* 7 no. (1) (2003): 11–19.

7. Berceli, D., T*he Revolutionary Trauma Release Process: Transcend Your Toughest Times.* Vancouver, Canada: Namaste, 2008.

8. Deuschl, G., Bain, P., Brin, M.; Ad Hoc Scientific Committee, Consensus statement of the Movement Disorder Society on tremor. *Movement Disorder* 13 (Suppl. 3) (1998): 2–23.

9. Wyne, K. T., "A Comprehensive Review of Tremor," *JAAPA* 18 no. (12) (2005): DSM 5.

10. Smaga, S., "Tremor," *American Family Physician* 68 no.8 (2003): 1546.

11. Cardinale, M., & Bosco, C., "The Use of Vibration as an Exercise Intervention," *The American College of Sports Medicine* 31 no. (1) (2003): 3–7.

12. Bosco, C., Colli, E., Introini, M., Cardinale, O., Tsarpela, A., Madella, J., Tihanyi, S., von Duvillard, A., & Viru, I., "Adaptive Responses of Human Skeletal Muscle to Vibration Exposure," *Clinical Physiology* 19 (1999): 183–187.

13. Berceli, D., "Evaluating the Effects of Stress Reduction Exercises Employing Mild Tremors: A Pilot Study" (Doctoral Thesis, Arizona State University, 2007).

14. Berceli, D., *Trauma Releasing Exercises: A Revolutionary New Method for Stress/trauma Recovery.* Charleston, S.C: Create Space Publishers, 2005.

15. Ross A, Thomas S. "The Health Benefits of Yoga and Exercise: A Review of Comparison Studies," *Journal of Alternative and Complementary Medicine* 16 no. (1) (2010): 3–12.

16. Padmini, T., Chametcha, S., Hongasandra, N., & Nagarathna, R., "Effect of Short-Term Intensive Yoga Program on Pain, Functional Disability and Spinal Flexibility in Chronic Low Back Pain: A Randomized Control Study," *Journal of Alternative and Complementary Medicine* 14 no. (6) (2008): 637–44. doi:10.1089/acm.2007.0815.

17. Kirkwood, G., Rampes, H, Tuffrey, V., Richardosn, J. Pilkington, K., Ramaratnam, S., "Yoga for Anxiety: A Systematic Review of the Research," *British Journal of Sports Medicine* 39 no. 12 (2005): 884–91.

18. Sander, M., "Medical Applications of Qigong," *Alternative Therapies* 2 no. (1) (1996).

19. Kuramoto, A., "Therapeutic Benefits of Tai Chi Exercise: Research Review," *Wisconsin Medical Journal* 105 no. 7 (2006): 40–46.

20. Kabat-Zinn, J., *Mindfulness Meditation: Cultivating the Wisdom of Your Body and Mind.* Simon & Schuster, NY, NY. 2002.

21. Simon & Schuster, NY, NY. 2002.

22. Napoli, M., *Tools for Mindful Living: Steppingstones for Practice.* Dubuque, IO: Kendall Hunt Publishers, 2010.

23. Berceli, D., & Napoli, M., "A Proposal for a Mindfulness-Based Trauma-Prevention Program for Social Work Professionals," *Complementary Health Practice Review* 11 no. (3) (2006): 153–65.

KNOWLEDGE LEARNED

1. Can you name the two primary parts of the nervous system?

_____

_____

_____

_____

2. The autonomic or involuntary nervous system is divided into two main categories. Can you name them?

_____

_____

_____

_____

3. Which part of the nervous system excites the body for the fight-or-flight response, and which part of the nervous system calls the body down for the rest-and-relaxation response?

_____

_____

_____

_____

4. From which part of the body does the nervous system receive its greatest amount of sensory input?

_____

_____

_____

_____

5. The myofascia is divided into two components. Can you name them?

_____

_____

_____

_____

6. What are the three major components of yoga practice?

_____

_____

_____

_____

7. What is the primary concept of qigong?

_____

_____

_____

_____

8. What are the self-defense qualities that are unique to tai chi?

_____

_____

_____

_____

9. What are the two most important components of mindfulness meditation?

_____

_____

_____

_____

MINDFUL AWARENESS REFLECTION JOURNAL

Choose one mindful experience as you begin your reflection.

 ### *Empathically Acknowledge*

Describe your experience

_____

_____

_____

 ### *Intentional Attention*

Describe what you noticed

Breath
Body
Emotions
Thoughts
Senses

 ### *Accept Without Judgment*

Describe judgment; acceptance

_____

_____

_____

 ### *Willingly Choose*

Intention/willingness; new perspective

_____

_____

_____

 ### *Mindful Mac Meditation*

Describe your meditation experiences. What did you learn?

_____

_____

_____

CHAPTER CRITICAL THINKING AND ACTIVITY JOURNAL

This is an opportunity for you to fully describe your thoughts, opinions and experience following the reading and activities.

The most important information/key concepts we need to understand from these chapters are:

_____

_____

_____

_____

How can I use the information in the chapters to help me with my daily mindfulness practice?

_____

_____

_____

_____

In what ways will the material learned in these chapters help me manage my stress more effectively?

_____

_____

_____

_____

What are your thoughts and feedback regarding the information and activities for each chapter?

_____

_____

_____

_____

CHAPTER THREE

WHOLE PERSON HEALTH ACROSS THE LIFE SPAN

By Steven Peterson

Photograph courtesy of Maria Napoli

"We begin life with our first breath and end with our last
Make every breath and every experience
Add love and laughter to your life"

Maria Napoli

What Is Whole Person Health?

"When I want foliage to protect me from those bitter winter days;
or a canopy of shade to block the sun's hot rays;
I want something big and strong;
with deep, healthy roots that will last a lifetime long;
Beautiful yet able to withstand all opposing powers;
with powerful limbs covered in lush green leaves and flowers.
I will be meticulous as I nurture my tree;
so why shouldn't I be as meticulous with me?"

This morning as I sat on my patio relishing the crispness in the air and the abundance of trees and flowers as far as my eye could see, I felt calm. The slight breeze wafting every unique fragrance of flora and fauna was soothing. The cup of tea in my hand was warm and refreshing. I truly felt as if there was no more perfect moment than now. Then gradually sprinklers came on and introduced a brisk moisture into this perfect moment. Suddenly the air was more crisp, the fragrants more pronounced, the greens and colors more vivid, and even my tea was more aromatic. The simple addition of one fundamental and critical element for all of life to thrive was reintroduced and intensified the perfection of an already perfect moment. And I was even more calm.

Now imagine, if you will, my patio experience abruptly ending with lawn mowers and hedge trimmers. Loud trucks and leaf blowers. Dust being stirred instead of sprinklers. The calmness would have ended with the closing of a patio door and being relegated to the inside of my house.

I could react to the industrial stimulus and carry that negative stressor into my day; or I could respond to the interruption by going back outside when it is over and watering the trees and plants and flowers, adding moisture to settle the dust and recreating pronounced fragrance and vivid colors. While holding my fresh cup of tea.

The key element here is: We all have the power to create the perfect, calming moment by understanding three very crucial tenets:

1. Be mindful of, and receptive to, the positive influence of the simplest of elements in your natural surroundings,
2. Not only refuse to let a stressor ruin a calming, positive moment, but also insist on recreating that moment once the stressor has been removed, and
3. Never lose sight that your calming, positive moment is very simple, easily attainable and always at your disposal.

As we explore whole person health, it is important to be mindful of these tenets as they are applied throughout the lifespan. The application spans from prenatal care into infancy, though adulthood and onward into our elderly years. There is the contribution of positive influences and the contamination of negative repercussions. Are you contributing? Or contaminating?

Consider this: Meticulous care is given to a newborn by their mother. Similarly attention is given to the prosperity and health of the elderly. What happens in-between those milestones that causes us, as individuals and a society, to lose sight of that? Is it any less important to care for ourselves with the same passion and commitment during those 80-plus years? Of course not. . . . but we need to learn to be mindful of the specific developmental stages and the impact that positive and negative influences have on healthy growth and living. Take the first step today. We do not have to revisit the past to make a positive effect on our future. Let there be no judgment of your past; only validation of your future.

A Jar Full of Nickels

If someone were to ask you for a nickel, you probably wouldn't think twice about giving them one.

Conversely, if someone handed YOU a nickel, you would be remiss about its relevance.

Now start collecting all of the nickels you encounter and put them in a jar.

Once the jar is full, would you give someone all of your nickels?

Personal stress is like a nickel.

A few is hardly noticeable, but a jar is a lot.

Don't wait until the jar is full before you notice your nickels.

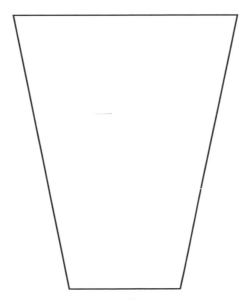

Fill this jar with the top ten nickels you currently possess

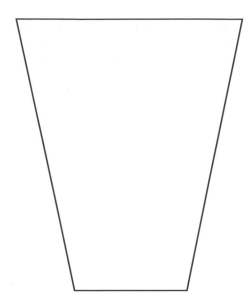

Now identify five of those nickels that you can eliminate from your life in the next thirty days and place them in this jar

Image © Vasilyev Alexandr, 2014. Used under license from Shutterstock, Inc.

In the Beginning— Before You are Born

There are numerous well-known biomedical effects that carry from the mother to her unborn child (substance abuse, alcohol consumption, cigarette smoking, dietary considerations, etc.). Prenatal care is, essentially, lifelong physiological and mental preparation. Aside from genetic dispositions/ disorders, the transient effects of stress and diet are evident in the unborn fetus.[1] Studies indicate a correlation between stress and anxiety levels of pregnant women and the effects on the fetus. Specifically spontaneous abortion, preterm labor, malformed or growth-retarded babies, unfavorable child development, and long-term functional disorders.[1]

Often overlooked from an empirical perspective is the permanent engraving that *in utero* programming has on everyone. This engraving uncovers itself later in life (be it at age one, in adolescence or early adulthood) not unlike an ancient scripture is uncovered as winds blow sand from its surface.

Let us revisit our "jar full of nickels" for a moment. If we examine a 5-foot 4-inch woman who weighs 131 pounds that carries with her ONE stressor throughout her pregnancy, the effect of that stressor is equivalent to her new born child holding SEVENTEEN nickel's worth of stress at the time of birth.[1] Imagine not having a mindful and healthy pregnancy and shouldering the burden of stress that equates

---

[1]Computation based on the 5 gram weight of a nickel, a 5-foot 4-inch preterm female with a medium frame weight of 131 pounds (59,421 grams), and an average birth weight of 7.5 pounds (3,402 grams). A factor of 17.465 used to compute the proportionate weight of a nickel on a newborn child.

to a jar full of nickels? Even if mom's stress is tacit, the explicit effects on her baby are unfathomable. Conversely, mom can impart unto her unborn child SEVENTEEN nickel's worth of *lifelong positive characteristics, developmental strengths and healthy habits* for every ONE mindful act she practices herself! Such powerful and selfless acts not only have an immediate healthful effect on mom, but also cement the foundation from which her unborn child will catapult forward throughout their life.

Write Your Birthplan

Don't plan on giving your child everything you never had.

Instead give your child everything you have during the first nine months of their life.

Identify some "best practices" that a mother can do to affect a positive and healthy birth for her child. Be specific:

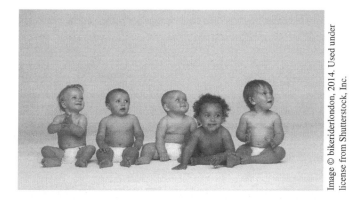

Image © bikeriderlondon, 2014. Used under license from Shutterstock, Inc.

Infancy—Introduction to a Healthy World

You might think that infants are limited in the ability to connect to what is happening outside of themselves. It is not surprising since they seem self-centered and demand to have their needs met when they cry, yet they are constantly communicating with others responding to touch, facial expression, moods, emotions, and energy of those around them and the environment. Infants are emotional sponges. Their level of receptivity is not unlike that of an animal. Everyone has heard that animals can sense fear and excitement. This is because everyone (humans and animals) increase specific chemical levels when they are in sympathetic mode—or "fight or flight" response. Cortisol is the primary stress hormone that floods the body during times of increased anxiety. Epinephrine (also known as adrenaline) serves a dual function as neurotransmitter and hormone and is responsible for the regulation of heart rate during sympathetic mode.[2] It is these two hormones that animal hypersensitivity can detect, and as such determines primal response to a perceived threat. Adults are less receptive to this sensitivity as we have developed other cognitive and relational tools to interact with animals and humans. Infants, however, develop with this hypersensitivity as they are still primal and unfiltered. Infants are more reactionary in this response because they have a very acute and limited sensory antenna.

Infant hearing is most mature at birth, while vision is the least developed. There are also the same auditory stress effects on an infant as an adult. Infants hear stressful voices, fighting, and other auditory overstimulation. Blood pressure increases, and cortisol gets released.[3] In a nutshell, infants will react to the same stress that an adult brings into their world. And this stress carries the same toll on their little bodies as it would on an adult: cortisol and epinephrine release. How do infants explicitly deal with this stress? By sleeping and crying.

The underlying importance of mindful parenting includes not only proper dietary considerations for the infant and removal of a stressful environment, but also physical nurturing. Isolation and sensory deprivation can harm brain development while an appropriately complex social network will enhance neurological growth.[4] Mindful parenting creates an empathetic emotional connection with the infant. When there is active attention and focus on the needs and responses of the infant, this selfless parental direction provides not only physical comfort but also unspoken emotional growth. Not unlike all animals, when attention is not being directed there is a sense of abandonment. Emotional damage will manifest itself through uncontrolled emotional response (anger) or being overly frightened of normal events and experiences. Infants require love and stimulation as early deprivation results in increased mental, emotional, and physiological impairment the longer the stress[5] (yes stress . . . as deprivation causes physiological stress on an infant) continues. This positive connectivity relies heavily on reinforcement—ongoing and consistent reinforcement. Infant memory may be quite fragile, but it is far from absent.

There is another interesting component to infant healthy development: they respond to motion. Parents soothe and quiet their infant by "rocking" and other patterned movements. A healthy dose of consistent, yet appropriate, "rocking" sets a physiological and neurological pattern against sedentary activity. Even at our earliest age we are programmed for exercise and activity.[6] Fostering this tacit developmental component can provide a foundation for future disposition to healthy active living!

Finally, it is important to understand an invisible developmental manifestation that is occurring: the immune system. The infant's immune system starts its peak development by two to three months, and reaches full development by the age of 11–14. The highest receptive physiological point of immune development is age 4–6 where catch-up vaccinations can be administered as well as subsequent doses following initial vaccination, according to the Centers for Disease Control 2013 Immunization Schedule. Stress—physical and mental—is one of the most detrimental events to an immune system. Adults under a great deal of stress experience a weakened immune system that manifests in lethargy, cold, sicknesses, etc. However, adults can address the stressor and take steps to rebuild their impaired immune system. Infants are at the foundational stage of their immune system development. Once established, there is no "do-over." It is of paramount importance that infants receive a healthy, peaceful, and mindful environmental stimulus—because the long-term effects of an impaired and suppressed immune system are irreparable. Flip the coin: if their fragile immune systems are nurtured, the long-term benefits are without question.

Social-Environmental Impact

Infants rely on olfactory and auditory hypersensitivity—and respond accordingly
(sympathetic or parasympathetic response).

Bringing positive energy—mindful parenting—around an infant will have the same powerful,
yet healthy, impact on them as would the less-desirable stress response.

If you had an infant in your arms at this very moment, what would you do in the next ten minutes to be a mindful parental figure? Answer in top half of circle.

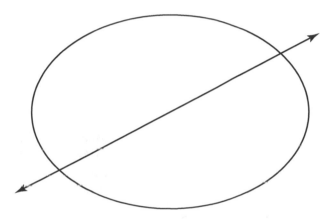

If you had one year to prepare for that infant in your arms, what would you plan on doing to be a mindful parental figure? Answer in bottom half of circle.

Toddlers to Childhood: Branching Out on Their Own

This is a powerful and magical discovery for the developing child. An age of omnipotence—every input, stimulus, sight, sound, smell, taste, and experience is pouring over the child and absorbed without prejudice. This "sensory magnetism" is the beginning of experience integration. In other words, this is the period where children link sensory

experiences with formal cognitive constructs. Also a period where habits are learned and practiced without judgment or consequential awareness.

There is an explosion of synaptic growth and the beginning of what we call "hard-wiring" in the brain. The brain develops in two distinct stages: the limbic system and the prefrontal cortex. The first to develop are the instinctual and emotional responses. A child's emotional impulses, selfishness, risk-taking, and primitive motivation are demonstrated early in life as the limbic system develops. As the child develops, the prefrontal cortex (gray matter) starts its growth spurt. Referred to as "reflective" intelligence, the prefrontal cortex is responsible for thought differentiation, response inhibition, social control, and emotional regulation. Early childhood is a period where learning is very malleable and adaptive, but there is poor impulse control. Not until the prefrontal cortex starts developing can unregulated emotion be tempered and all of the pieces of the learning puzzle slowly come to fruition.[7] The unique characteristic about this explosive neural growth is that it is sporadically focused and mostly random, rampant primal learning. This environmental education is a flood of input from everything in their surroundings. Remember the last time you were at a shopping mall? When a lot of young children were running around?

"Jeffrey! Come here! Jeffrey. . . . stop running! Come back here, Jeffrey! Jeffrey get out of people's way! Stop climbing in the plants! Jeffrey! Get away from the water fountain! Leave the nice lady alone, Jeffrey! Jeffrey. . . put that down! Don't put that in your mouth! Jeffrey!"

All the while Jeffrey is running with all of his might. Not looking straight ahead, mind you! He is visually targeting everything other than the direction in which he is traveling. He is absorbing absolutely every piece of input he possibly can. You are now keenly aware of Jeffrey's presence. Suddenly Jeffrey is in front of you . . . then behind you . . . then next to you . . . then talking to you . . . . then he's behind you again . . . then he's running a mad dash across all lanes of pedestrian traffic . . . then he's suddenly under your feet . . . then he's climbing on the vendor kiosk because he see's something shiny. You have just experienced sixty seconds in young Jeffrey's day!

Now mindfully observe all of this hectic activity. (Kindly ignore the mom or dad who is having a mental meltdown . . . whose voice has reached an octave one above that of an opera singer). You are witnessing, first-hand, this explosive synaptic growth and environmental education.

Appreciate how young Jeffrey is learning and what he is filling his brain with. Understand that this unscripted chaos is vital to his mental development. This is a crucial stage in young Jeffrey's life because this is where good habits need to be hardwired in his brain. Without a mindful, parental presence throughout this age of discovery, bad habits (or worse, nonhabits) will be part of his new circuitry.

As the child is lead and learns to healthfully integrate all of these new experiences, his ego starts to form. The child's sense of self and personal identity is realized when positive behaviors are reinforced and negative behaviors are quelled. Notice the word, "punished," was not used. At this age failure to provide positive reinforcement for undesirable behavior can elicit a healthy patterned response. Depending on the circumstance and situation, punishment can certainly be warranted.

Understand that when it comes to reinforcing and promoting positive healthy behaviors, children only know what they are taught. Cognitive processing comes later. A child can neither process nor articulate good versus bad habits/behaviors until after they have been taught, through modeling, what the desirable behaviors are.[8,9] Many of us have had a puppy in our lives that we had to train. It serves comparatively little purpose to punish the puppy when it does something wrong versus rewarding the puppy when it does something good. We reward appropriate behavior, and as such the puppy actively seeks to demonstrate the positive behavior instead or doing something wrong because it wants the loving validation and avoidance of negativity. With time there is no choice but to demonstrate healthy, positive behavior. Reinforcement of negativity will imprint itself on the child's synaptic circuit as strongly as positivity. So instead mindfully focus on what TO do, instead of what NOT to do.

Positive Reinforcement

"The way positive reinforcement is carried out is more important than the amount."

B. F. Skinner

If you could teach a child three things that YOU feel would be of most benefit to their lives, what would they be?

1)

2)

3)

Amazing Adolescence

Image © 1000 Words, 2014. Used under license from Shutterstock, Inc.

"I am a teenager.
I fall in love too fast.
I forgive too easily.
I crash too hard.
I care too much."

Unknown

The adolescent years are an incredible experiential and learning period. This is the point in our lives where we have flashes of intellectual brilliance tempered by unregulated emotion. An adolescent is defining the world through their intellectual and social discoveries. To put a chronological structure on this period, we will define adolescence as puberty into young adulthood (early twenties).

Why early twenties? To fully appreciate and mindfully nurture the cognitive and social-developmental brain of an adolescent, it is important to understand how two opposing forces (the Limbic System and Prefront Cortex) develop.

The Limbic System is the first to develop and is the center for instinctual and emotional reaction. Commonly referred to as "the social brain," this area is responsible for emotional impulses, selfishness, risk-taking behavior and primitive motivation. This area of the brain does not change with time and is formative.

The prefrontal cortex is not fully matured until about the age of twenty-five. This is the "reflective brain" and is where we find the hardwired skills of thought differentiation, response inhibition, emotional regulation, prediction of outcomes, social control, and organization. This part of the brain is the "gray matter" that actually develops over time and is able to be formed by learning and experience.[10] It is evident that the adolescent mind is constantly at opposition with itself.

Adolescents are very malleable and adaptive, yet they have poor impulse control. They tend to be unaware of the implications their actions have on others and are constantly conflicted between their perception and the perception of others.[11] This is the age where we see teenage boys ride a skateboard off a second floor balcony and try to land on a stair railing positioned five feet away from oncoming traffic.

LIMBIC SYSTEM STRUCTURES

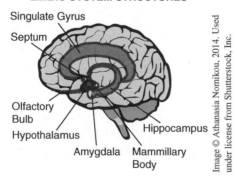

Singulate Gyrus
Septum
Olfactory Bulb
Hypothalamus
Amygdala
Hippocampus
Mammillary Body

Image © Athanasia Nomikou, 2014. Used under license from Shutterstock, Inc.

"Hey! Check this out!" is the thought process instead of, "What is the possibility of me winding up in a hospital?" Limbic versus prefrontal.

In short, the mental and sensory stimulus that the average adolescent experience is very stressful and often unhealthy. Adolescents lack the experience and coping mechanisms to make mindful, healthy decisions as they grapple with this tumultuous yet transient period.

At this very time there is also an explosion of synaptic growth that is unparalleled throughout the rest of our lives. This is a small window of an incredible learning opportunity that quickly closes as we progress into adulthood.

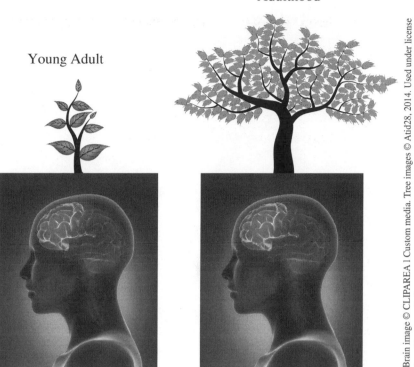

Adolescence

Young Adult

Adulthood

How the adolescent progresses through this stage of their lives dictates their own identity development—not just their own self-esteem and personal awareness, but also their own sexual awareness. How their sexual identity fit into not only their immediate and familial environment, but also how fulfill that role into adulthood. Socioeconomic as well as cultural demands require a strong sense of identity and tools to respond to those demands.

The personal and social skills that an adolescent learns cement themselves and pave the highway for lifelong adult decision-making. Supplanting healthy and mindful habits for not only health and welfare, but also social and personal leadership, will be the foundation for the next generation of children that these soon-to-be-young adults will be bringing into the world.

As the prefrontal cortex reaches full maturity the cooperative regulation of the Limbic System will determine how healthy the adult coping mechanisms will be coping with stress, life experiences, decision-making, etc. Taking full advantage of the synaptic explosion and monopolizing this opportunity for efficacious learning is a wonderful period of life! A healthy and mindful adolescent will be a healthy and mindful adult. It is this adult that will begin the cycle of whole person health.

Adolescents Employ a Different Cognitive Strategy than Do Adults

The adolescents are determining their sense of identity, are defining their self-efficacy, lack a support system, and have a need for acceptance and need to build their self-esteem.

Be cognizant and mindful of this amazing, yet fragile, period of their lives.

Today is the first blank page of a 365-page book . . . help them write a good one.

Identify the five most important lessons you learned during your adolescence:

1)

2)

3)

4)

5)

Identify the five greatest challenges you faced during your adolescence:

1)

2)

3)

4)

5)

If you could do it over again, what would you change about your adolescence?

Young Adulthood

Young adulthood is the period of newly acquired social, emotional, fiscal, and emotional responsibilities. This is a tremendously defining period in all of our lives. In essence, the stage is being set for how we will carry out the rest of our time on this earth.

For most, this is the first time choices had to be made outside of the parent's home or a collegiate environment, which means from this point forward choices are no longer being made for us. We have to shoulder the responsibility and accountability for life-directing and life-altering decisions. The decisions made from the mid-twenties to early thirties carry the greatest personal impact with respect to financial budgeting, planning for a professional and/or family future, gender roles, relationship decisions, socioeconomic constraints and socialization/resocialization. All of these defining moments set the course for happiness or duress for many decades to come. And often, there are no "do-overs."

Clearly, the heaviest life decisions are made during this developmental period. What is even clearer is the opportunity for health-debilitating stress-related events. The greater the decision and responsibility, the greater the risk for the body to fall into its sympathetic response mode.[12]

Additionally, there is another unique shift in inter- and intrapersonal relationships that has not existed in previous generations: social media. Technology is the primary medium of communication for the current generation. As such, we are seeing a reduction in interpersonal direct communication.[13] This lack of face-to-face interaction creates its own unique stressor. From daily communications through text messaging and instant messaging to online dating, human interaction is being replaced with words and pictures on a screen. This elevates levels of expectations and misinformation/miscommunication. The art of reading facial expressions, body movements, and direct contact has taken a back seat to deciphering a text, creating an emoticon or conveying a statement through a very impersonal and sterile electronic medium. Relationships are created and ended this way, schoolyard hazing has become cyberbullying and workplace supervisory actions have become an email attachment.

Although there is a tremendous increase in the ability to communicate through electronic media, there is the risk of creating that safety net of saying whatever is on one's mind without scripting as one would during face-to-face communication.

Of paramount importance for this age group is not only the acquisition, but also transference of, mindful and healthy coping skills in order to effectively navigate these new life challenges.

The body has a built-in mechanism for preventing the debilitating effects of stress: laughter. Dopamine is the major component of the brain's system of seeking reward upon release, dopamine reinforces pleasure-seeking behavior and influences happiness.

When we laugh, our brain releases these "feel good" chemical into our bodies. In addition, laughter floods our bodies with endorphins (opiates capable of pain relief, not unlike a sedative narcotic), and growth hormone (necessary for not only tissue growth, but also metabolism). These substances have broad psychological effects that include decreasing blood pressure and bolstering our immune systems.[14]

Remember that the body goes into sympathetic response mode during times of stress. During this "fight or flight" mode, adrenaline (epinephrine), norepinephrine, and cortisol enter the bloodstream. These are the major stress hormones.[15] Laughter triggers the body's parasympathetic response mode and the release of dopamine.[16]

The human body cannot be in sympathetic and parasympathetic response modes at the same time. As such, the body cannot release stress hormones and dopamine at the same time! If one is laughing, they physiologically cannot be stressed out!

Stressful situations can be diffused with laughter. Before engaging in a confrontation with a significant other, coworker, or careless driver, invoke laughter in some manner. An intense, negative conversation quells the release of dopamine.

Consider this: cell phone conversations during motor vehicle operation. If not a casual or happy conversation, the only other cell phone conversations conducted behind the wheel of an automobile would be of an intense or negative nature which would indicate the driver is experiencing stress hormone release. Visual and auditory acuity is hindered, reflexive and motor skills are hampered. The driver is neither fully physically nor mentally equipped to operate a motor vehicle.[17] The presence of a hands-free device does not diminish the effects of their sympathetic response mode.

Engage in laughter whenever possible. Your body cannot tote the baggage of stress when a smile is the first thing to enter the room.

Laughter. . . .

What have you done for fun (something that made you very happy and laugh out loud) this past week?

List three fun activities (including happiness and laughter) that you will accomplish next week?

1)

2)

3)

Image © ollyy, 2014. Used under license from Shutterstock, Inc.

Middle to Older Adulthood

This is the point in life where decisions are made that will carry us into our senior years. Long-term career planning and decisions about retirement tend to be the focal point as we enter our forties. Stable relationships contribute to the success of this planning— partner expectations, familial dependency, and interdependence can ultimately provide strength and peace of mind.

During adulthood individual lives are continuing to build upon the foundation previously set forth, with increased focus on career and family. A sense of accomplishment allows adults to feel secured and that they are an active contributing member to home and community. Failure to feel this sense of accomplishment tends to lead to feelings of inferiority and social noninvolvement. Having pride in life accomplishments (watching children and family grow, unity with life partner, etc.) is of paramount importance.[18] Lack of which can lead to increased health concerns, substance abuse, and depression.

A study conducted over a ten-year period indicates the percentage of adults aged 65 and over with both hypertension and diabetes increased from 9 percent to 15 percent; prevalence of hypertension and heart disease increased from 18 percent to 21 percent; and prevalence of hypertension and cancer increased from 8 percent to 11 percent.[19]

In essence, a healthy successful transition through adulthood will have its greatest initial effect on mental wellness ultimately manifesting in physical health which is of great importance as this is the point in life where disease states and health concerns will start to appear.

Continuing whole person health into the senior years can be accompanied by a renewed sense of youthful vigor. Active late adult lifestyles has increased due not only to the overt health and wellness benefits—prevention of illness by including exercise and nutrition—but also because the socioeconomic dynamic has changed for senior citizens.[20] Retirement should not mean inactivity. Opportunities for volunteering or even second and third careers emerge as an option. Travel, activity groups, and social networks keep the mind and body in healthy, homeostatic state. Healthy, active senior living reduces the dependency upon their children to provide care and can delay (if not eliminate) the need for long-term hospice care.

Image © S. M. Beagle, 2014. Used under license from Shutterstock, Inc.

What is important is that we enter this phase in our lives with a positive reflection on our life's work, worth, and accomplishments. There should be no regrets, feelings of despair, or bitterness.[18]

And thus the cycle goes full circle. The wisdom and experience of age will parlay into leading and educating the upcoming generations of the importance of physical and mental health and well-being.

The benefits of whole person health are best demonstrated, not talked about.
It is best practiced, not anecdotal.
It is best taught by those who have lived it to the fullest.

Make Every Moment Count

"In the end, it's not the years in your life that count. It's the life in your years."

Abraham Lincoln

References

1. Mulder, E. J., Robles de Medina, P. G., Huizink, A. C., Van den Bergh, B. R., Buitelaar, J. K., & Visser, G. H., "Prenatal Maternal Stress: Effects on Pregnancy and the Unborn Child," *Early Human Development* 70, no. 1–1 (2002): 3–14.

2. Moore, R. Y., & Bloom F. E., "Central Catecholamine Neuron Systems: Anatomy and Physiology of the Norepinephrine and Epinephrine Systems," *Annual Review of Neuroscience* 1 (1978): 129–69.

3. Devereux, R. B., Pickering, T. G., Harshfield, G. A., Kleinert, H. D., Denby, L., Clark, L., Pregibon, D., Jason, M., Kleiner, B., Borer J. S., Laragh, J. H., "Left Ventricular Hypertrophy in Patients with Hypertension: Importance of Blood Pressure Response to Regularly Recurring Stress," *American Heart Association* 68 (1983):470–76.

4. Rubin, K. H., Coplan, Robert J., & Julie C. Bowker, Julie C., "Social Withdrawal in Childhood," *Annual Review of Psychology* 60 (2009): 141–71.

5. Izard, Carroll E., Fine, Sarah, Mostow, Allison, Trentacosta, Christopher, & Campbell, Jan., "Emotion Processes in Normal and Abnormal Development and Preventive Intervention," *Development & Psychopathology* 14 (2002): 761–87.

6. Adolph, K. E., "Motor and Physical Development: Locomotion." In *Encyclopedia of Infant and Early Childhood Development* edited by M. M. Haith & J. B. Benson, 359–73, San Diego, CA: Academic Press, 2008.

7. Johnson, Mark H., with Michelle de Haan, *Developmental Cognitive Neuroscience* (3rd ed.) (Wiley: 2011).

8. Morris, Amanda Sheffield, Silk, Jennifer S, Steinberg, Laurence, Myers, Sonya S., & Robinson, Lara Rachel., "The Role of the Family Context in the Development of Emotion Regulation," *Social Development* 16 (2007): 361–88.

9. Nielsen, Mark, "Copying Actions and Copying Outcomes: Social Learning Through the Second Year," *Developmental Psychology* 42 (2006): 555–65.

10. Popper, K. R., Eccles, J. C., John, C., & Carew, J., *The Self and Its Brain,* vol. 977. Berlin: Springer International, 1977, 362.

11. Pulkkinen, L. "Self-control and Continuity from Childhood to Late Adolescence," *Life-span Development and Behavior* 4 (1982): 63–105.

12. Dacey, John, Fiori, Lisa, "Stress in Adulthood," *Handbook of Human Development for Health Care Professionals*, 2006, 219. McGraw-Hill Humanities/Social Sciences/Languages; 7 edition (April 7, 2008)

13. Purcell, K., Smith, A., & Zickuhr, K., *Social Media & Mobile Internet Use Among Teens and Young Adults*. Washington, DC: Pew internet & American life project, 155–79, 2010.

14. Carter, S., "The Natural High of Laughter". *Laughter: A Remedy for Stress,* 2011.

15. Glick, G., Braunwald, E., Lewis, R., "Relative Roles of the Sympathetic and Parasympathetic Nervous Systems in the Reflex Control of Heart Rate," *Circulation Research* 16 (1965): 363–75.

16. Ziegler, J., "Immune System May Benefit from the Ability to Laugh," *Journal of National Cancer Institute* 87 (1995): 342–43.

17. Horrey, W., & Wickens, C., "Examing the Impact of Cell Phone Conversations on Driving Using Meta-Analytic Techniques," *Human Factors: The Journal of the Human Factors and Ergonomics Society* 48 (2006): 1196–205.

18. Erickson, Erik H., *The Life Cycle Completed: A Review*. New York, NY: Norton, 1982.

19. Freid, V. M., Bernstein, A. B., & Bush, M. A., *Multiple Chronic Conditions Among Adults Aged 45 and Over: Trends Over the Past 10 Years. NCHS Data Brief, No 100*. Hyattsville, MD: National Center for Health Statistics, 2012.

20. Katz, S., "Busy Bodies: Activity, Aging, and the Management of Everyday Life," *Journal of Aging Studies* 14, no. 2, (2000): 135–52.

QUESTIONS WORKSHEET

1. What are the three tenets of whole person health?

2. Identify three negative impacts stress can have on the unborn child?

3. What is the primary stress hormone that flood the body during times of increased anxiety?

4. Which is the dual-function chemical that is responsible for regulation of heart rate during "fight or flight" mode?

5. Impulsiveness, risk-taking and unregulated emotion are characteristics of the development of what part of the brain?

6. "Reflective Intelligence" develops when which part of the brain develops?

7. During which developmental period is synaptic growth in the brain at its greatest?

8. Which ANS (autonomic nervous system) response is what is characterized as the stress response?

MINDFUL AWARENESS REFLECTION JOURNAL

4 Step **MAC** Guide

Choose one mindful experience as you begin your reflection.

Empathically Acknowledge

Describe your experience

_____

_____

_____

Intentional Attention

Describe what you noticed

Breath
Body
Emotions
Thoughts
Senses

Accept Without Judgment

Describe judgment; acceptance

_____

_____

_____

Willingly Choose

Intention/willingness; new perspective

_____

_____

_____

Mindful Mac Meditation

Describe your meditation experiences. What did you learn?

_____

_____

_____

CHAPTER CRITICAL THINKING AND ACTIVITY JOURNAL

This is an opportunity for you to fully describe your thoughts, opinions and experience following the reading and activities.

The most important information/key concepts we need to understand from these chapters are:

_____

_____

_____

_____

How can I use the information in the chapters to help me with my daily mindfulness practice?

_____

_____

_____

_____

In what ways will the material learned in these chapters help me manage my stress more effectively?

_____

_____

_____

_____

What are your thoughts and feedback regarding the information and activities for each chapter?

_____

_____

_____

_____

CHAPTER FOUR

SUSTAINABLE LIVING AND CONSCIOUS EATING

By Lisa Schmidt

Photograph courtesy of Maria Napoli

I am nourished by the earth
My food is alive with nutrients
My senses are ignited
My body is satisfied.

Maria Napoli

Photograph courtesey of Maria Napoli.

"The most effective diet is one eaten in the context of the principles that sustain the Tree of Life itself. This model for conscious living of a spiritual life includes meditation and/or prayer; cultivation of wisdom; good fellowship with other conscious people; right livelihood; respect for the Earth and its inhabitants; love of the family and all humanity; respect for all people and cultures; respect for the forces of Mother Nature; respect and love for our own body and mind; and love for the overall totality of who we are. "

—Dr. Gabriel Cousens, *Conscious Eating*[1] The Tree of Life.[1]

The following chapter will offer you an opportunity to reflect on the food you eat, where it comes from, how you eat, and what happens in your body the moment you take a mouthful. Your eating experience will most likely change for life as you mindfully acknowledge what your current patterns of nutrition; pay attention how you choose the food you eat and when you eat; accept your experiences and decisions without judgment and finally take action to make a choice for change. Be gentle with yourself and take time to absorb the information shared with you in "sustainable living for conscious eating" as you will most likely find that change needs to take place in your life, yet we mindfully need to take small steps as we become aware of the changes we need to make, take time to practice and develop new behaviors and attitudes toward our nutrition and finally, begin to integrate healthy and nutritious behaviors that will improve the quality of our lives. Let the journey begin!

Food has energetic properties, and learning how to use its effects to enhance health and well-being is an age-old practice. From the origins of mankind, hunter-gatherers learned about local plants, and knew which were edible and how to use others as medicine. This type of knowledge about plants and their medicinal uses formed the basis of Western herbal traditions and traditional Asian medical systems. However, the seventeenth century brought the Western view of man as machine and the body as subject to mechanical laws. Under this conceptual framework where Newtonian physics and pre-evolutionary biology project a mechanical view into a microscopic realm, the wisdom of food as medicine was lost in the West. Mechanics work in explaining machines, but the body cannot be entirely explained with this metaphor. In other traditions, the use of herbs and plants as medicine remains alive and vital. With a four thousand year tradition of food as medicine for humans, we can find written records of Ayurvedic and traditional Chinese medicine practices with time-proven protocols. Reclaiming this wisdom and melding it with modern nutrition knowledge help us choose foods that encourage healthful metabolic processes. This allows us to use plants in nutritionally healthful ways that form our connection to Nature and all living things.

Moving beyond man as machine and seeing all living beings as a part of Nature that is interconnected changes our view of food and the act of eating. Nourishment becomes much more than just about what you and your family ingest for dinner. It's also about the ripples that result from your need to eat, the entire world, and all of its inhabitants. We are all links in an enormous, complex food chain, and our lives depend upon our love and gratitude for all the other links. Buying organic spinach from a local farmer not only supports the farmer's family; it also supports microorganisms in the soil, plankton in water, and less junk in the landfill. Making conscious grocery store decisions support the sustainability of all living beings, and our collective futures.

When we remember that the Earth is the provider of our food, we learn how to eat consciously: awake, aware, and alive. No packaged product, protein powder, or laboratory formula can offer the same vitality and sustenance as Nature's direct offering. Nourished from within, we are able to give back to each other, our families, and our communities. As we sit down together and break bread in families, the food sharing ritual holds tremendous power. It is the spiritual glue that holds us together as families, friends, and communities.[2]

What we eat is linked to our awareness. Our food choices show our harmony (or lack of harmony) with ourselves, the world, and all of creation. The way we choose to eat and what we choose to eat makes us feel secure. This feeling of security makes it difficult, if not impossible, to change our diet unless presented with disease or pain associated with our current eating pattern. Many people are unwilling to make needed dietary or lifestyle changes even when their life depends on it.

Food as Energy

When we eat foods that are appropriate to our own individual needs we extract energy from our environment in harmony with the natural world. As we honor and respect our own body rhythms and eat in tune with our needs, we align with Nature and use food resources sustainably. Reducing waste, minimizing our carbon footprint, and maximizing finite resources, our bodies thrive. As we increase our connection to the process of eating and the world around us, we shift into harmony and make conscious lifestyle choices. We eat mindfully, consciously, and with love and affection for the Earth and ourselves.

Every day, we must meet the energy needs of our bodies despite fluctuations in the availability of the many nutrients the body needs. How do the cells of our bodies use fuel molecules, and what is involved in this process? The human body is dynamic and our cells have to switch between producing and using energy that we create from ingesting plants and animals. The body's ability to adapt in the face of always changing conditions is crucial, and only possible because of its ability to self-regulate. As our bodies move between different physiological conditions like sleeping through the night, we "break the fast" in the morning which requires the body to change into a different metabolic state. At other times, we might be simply resting, or exercising. In all situations, the type and amount of nutrients available as cellular fuel changes abruptly. In order to provide the energy the body needs, we eat a variety of food, which the body in its amazing process converts into the energy we need to live. Through eating, we transform plants and animals into mitochondria, called our "cellular power plants" because they generate most of the cell's supply of adenosine triphosphate (ATP). ATP is used as a source of chemical energy[3] by all plants and animals, fueling all life functions. In addition to supplying cellular energy, mitochondria are involved in other tasks such as signaling, cellular differentiation, cell death, as well as the control of the cell cycle and cell growth.[3]

Let's look at this transformation through the example of eating a tuna sandwich. How does our body accomplish this magic act of eating the mitochondria of plants and animals and converting them into our

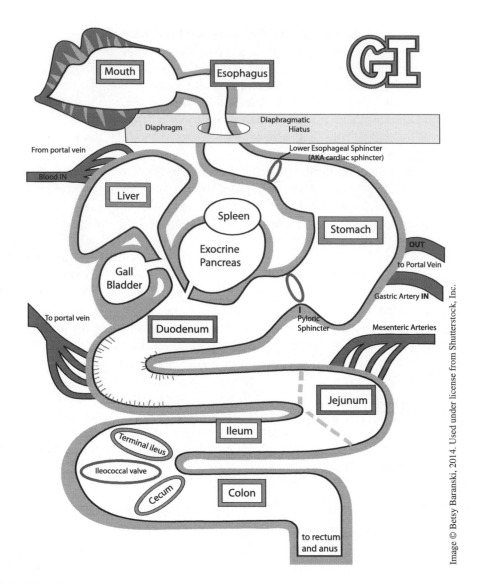

Image © Betsy Baranski, 2014. Used under license from Shutterstock, Inc.

The biochemical pathway of food—eating a Sandwich

own mitochondria? The process of conversion is accomplished through the body's process of digestion. Before we even begin the mechanical act of chewing, digestion begins in the mouth. Our salivary glands secrete fluid even when we think about eating, or smell food, or pick up the sandwich. This lubrication allows us to soften and break down the food for chewing, which grinds the sandwich into smaller particles (using the teeth), and saliva provides better interaction with taste receptors, making food more pleasurable to our senses. One type of saliva, salivary amylase, is slightly acidic, and it is perfectly adjusted pH helps break down starches from the sandwich (for example, the bread) and turns the complex starch molecules into single units—again, preparing the food for digestion. The mechanical (chewing) and chemical (amylase) process is the beginning of the metabolism of the tuna, mayonnaise, lettuce,

tomato, and bread—otherwise known as protein, fats, and carbohydrates. Let's take a walk through the food processing experience.

The bread—a primarily carbohydrate source of energy—starts to break down into simple sugar units which can be rapidly transported by our mitochondria across the intestinal wall and delivered quickly to body tissues. This classic conversion of plant mitochondria (from the bread) into our own mitochondria is delivered throughout the body in a singular sugar unit called glucose, an important energy source in all living organisms and a component of many carbohydrates. Fat in the form of mayonnaise begins its breakdown into lipids. Lipids are a group of naturally occurring molecules that include fats, waxes, sterols, fat-soluble vitamins (such as vitamins A, D, E, and K), monoglycerides, diglycerides, triglycerides, phospholipids, and others. The main jobs that lipids perform in the body include storing energy, acting as signaling messengers to other cells, and providing structure for cell membranes.[4]

Not only does fat in the mayonnaise break down into molecules that help facilitate essential functions in our bodies like nerve conduction, hormone synthesis, and neurological transmission, it also provides a delivery vehicle for taste. Calorie dense, fat delivers twice the energy—in the form of calories—as protein or carbohydrates. It is also very effective in delivering flavors to the brain, enhancing the way processed foods taste, and encourage in subtle ways of our desire for more.

Next comes our assimilation of the tuna, the protein product that our body breaks down into amino acids. As the building blocks of protein, amino acids are the building blocks of life itself. Take a mindful moment and imagine eating the tuna sandwich, paying attention to what is happening in your body as it is assimilated. We use amino acids following digestion to help the body break down food, grow, repair body tissue, and perform many other key functions. The body can also use them as a source of energy, but it is a less efficient fuel than using sugars. Every cell in the body contains protein. It is a major part of the skin, muscles, organs, and glands. Protein is also found in almost all body fluids. The tuna in the sandwich provides about ½ your daily protein requirement. It is from an animal source (fish)—but we can also get protein from plants. In fact, this sandwich provides protein in the tomato, lettuce, bread, and even the mayonnaise. You do not need to eat animal products to get all the protein you need in your diet.[5] The lettuce and tomato also begin breaking down into other kinds of carbohydrates:glucose and fructose.

What happens next to the broken down food? It moves by peristaltic waves stimulated by the nervous system to the stomach. Acid hydrolysis (hydrochloric acid, HCL) contributes to its degradation. HCL release is stimulated by a hormone called gastrin, which is released by the endocrine glands in the stomach in response to food; gastric releasing peptide (GRP), and the neurotransmitter acetylcholine.

HCL uncoils protein strands, and activates the stomach enzyme PEPSIN. Proteins from the tuna part of our sandwich are broken down into smaller molecules called polypeptides by the pepsin and HCL. The HCL changes the protein structure, and activates pepsinogen (another hormone), which activates the pepsin in the stomach. Pepsin cleaves ("cuts") proteins from large polypeptides into smaller polypeptides and frees amino acids. At the same time, the partially broken down fats are assimilated by the breakdown of their chemical structure into smaller units. Churning action of the stomach mixes the fat with water and the stomach acid, further breaking down the food into smaller and smaller units.

There isn't digestion happening in the stomach—so far, food is simply being broken down through this complex process into smaller and smaller usable units. In the stomach, only water and certain fat-soluble drugs are absorbed, as is alcohol. The sandwich keeps moving, and becomes acid chyme, moving further into the intestine for digestion. The sandwich is now liquefied, and passes into the duodenum, the first segment of the small intestine. Ten inches long, it performs the important function of neutralizing the liquid to the appropriate pH, protecting the sensitive epithelial tissue in the intestine from damage. More intestinal cells release digestive juices, which help to move nutrients from the liquefied food throughout the small intestine. The balance of pH is really important, and our bodies are designed to keep the pH at just the right levels. With pH calibrated, the pancreas releases amylase, CCK, and secretin (enzymes and hormones). The nervous system is involved too, and helps to control the right amount to complete the digestive process.

More splitting of polypeptides (proteins) continues as enzymes are activated. You could say that the small intestine completely liquefies and absorbs the proteins. A cascade of reactions involving other enzymes happens as the protein continues to degrade. Once the protein breaks down into the individual amino acids they pass through the walls of the intestine. These free amino acids are then distributed by the blood system to all the body's tissues, especially muscle, where they build back up again into proteins! Any extra amino acids are broken down by the liver, which is converted into glucose or fatty acids (stored in the body), with part of the amino acid excreted from the body as urine.

The full digestion of sugars leads to their absorption into the body and conversion by the liver and other tissues into fatty acids, amino acids, and glycogen. This process is less complicated for the body than digesting proteins. Sugars in the form of glycogen convert readily into energy, and have a big role in providing fuel to the body.

What happens to the fats? Their digestion and absorption relies upon bile and pancreatic secretions. When fat enters the SI, the gallbladder receives a signal to release bile to liquefy the fat. Bile's emulsifying action converts fat globules into smaller droplets that repel each other. Did you know what an important role your gallbladder plays? The myth that the gall bladder is an unnecessary organ is demystified here as we see its very significant role as the main liquefier of fat! Following the emulsification process, enzymes get easy access to fat droplets. The pancreas secretes other hormones, which release the fatty acid part of the lipid, breaking it down into usable components.

Small particles called micelles are formed. Fitting in between microvilli, the microscopic parts of cells that increase its surface area, the micelles then move products of fat digestion from the SI to the brush border of the intestine where they can be absorbed into the intestinal cells. Following their absorption, they are broken down into glycerol and fatty acids, which recombine into triglycerides. The triglycerides become incorporated into another transport vehicle called chylomicrons, which move into the lymphatic system. The chylomicrons then go to adipose tissue, muscle, and liver where the fats are deposited in the body for longer-term storage.

Anything left over from this amazing story will exit through the large intestine as feces. If all goes well, this final step removes indigestible fiber, some intestinal prokaryotes along for the ride, and bacteria. What a journey!

The Individual's Relationship to Food

The wonderful thing about food is you get three votes a day. Every one of them has the potential to change the world.

—Michael Pollan

Image © Simon Booth, 2014. Used under license from Shutterstock, Inc.

Food and Our Emotions

How have you noticed the central role food plays in your life? From the time we are born we are developing deep associations between food and our emotions. As infants, our cries are answered with mother's milk and Nature's design, which combines a complete experience of receiving physical food with emotional connection and safety. Finding ways to nurture healthy emotional connections while feeding our bodies is the ultimate nourishment. We spend our lives linking food to our emotional needs in ways that attempt to recreate that early experience. Culturally, food plays a central role in life's rituals. We celebrate occasions like weddings, holidays, graduations, and promotions, and food becomes a significant focus and strongly linked to emotions. Expressions like "drowning our sorrows," "power lunches," "chicken soup for the soul," and even "swallow your pride" demonstrate how we use food to express, suppress, and manage love and many other emotions.

In light of these factors, we have many mixed feelings about food. Experiencing extremes with food are not unusual, including dieting, stuffing, fasting, gorging, starving, cravings, and even the bingeing/purging of anorexia and bulimia. We are a nation where one third of the US population is significantly overweight, and more than one quarter-24 percent of adult males, 27 percent of adult females, and 27 percent of children—are obese.[6]

In one sense, overeating leading to excessive weight is a disease of affluence. However, multiple factors are at play that include changes in genetics, major innovations that cause us to move around less (the automobile, television), an abundant, cheap food supply that is nutrient poor, and changing through technology plants and animals designed to feed us in perfect harmony with Nature. This manipulation of foods into "food like substances" is suspected to have negatively impacted our health in ways that have profoundly affected our ability to remain within normal weight ranges.[7]

Concerns about physical health, heart disease, and cancer have increased awareness of the nutrients in our food—especially cholesterol, saturated fat, antioxidant vitamins—and the benefits of eating more of some foods and less of others. Our mounting health concerns has helped us realize how we have changed the way we eat. Trends in American eating habits in the past 100 years have dramatically reduced the amount of fresh, whole foods we eat and have increased our consumption of sugar, beef, cheese, and fats.

Any discussion of how food affects us is incomplete if we focus only on the nutritional quality of food. Food is more than just "nutrients." Progressive psychologists and nutrition professionals alike believe it is important to consider how we *feel* about the food we eat.[9] In addition to managing our health and weight through diet, food affects us in many mental, emotional, and spiritual ways. We fail to connect this with the food we eat; this lack of awareness leads to blind spots when we forget the connection that we have with plants and other living things. Have you considered whether your food is supporting you and how food affects your physical, mental, emotional, and spiritual health? Are you controlled by food, eating out of habit, or are you consciously eating to create the life you want? Let's explore how food affects you and your health—and how conscious eating can support your healing process and your creation of health and a dynamic, joyful life filled with energy and love.

Image © 2630ben, 2014. Used under license from Shutterstock, Inc.

Food as life—food IS life

Our ancestors were hunter-gatherers who never knew exactly where their next meal might be coming from. In fact, their "meals" were probably eaten on the run as they stalked enough prey to build an actual meal, but it is unlikely that their meals were regular or even eaten daily. Given the conditions under which food was obtained, it was impossible for them to take any of it for granted. Every morsel was hard-won and therefore, extremely precious, savored, and relished.

Over time, humans became more sedentary, transitioning from hunting and gathering to growing their own food. This agricultural advancement made eating more predictable as a result of a more stable lifestyle, and the energy expenditure to produce food resulted in few eating mindlessly. Whether living in a small agricultural village along the Nile River in ancient times or growing food in one's backyard garden in the twenty-first century, small-scale agriculture is physically demanding, and appreciation for food is made more special by the energy expended in growing it. Until as recently as 100 years ago, the human diet was compatible with the intelligent design of the human digestive system—low in fat, high in protein, complex carbohydrates and fiber, with no refined sugar. This fresh, whole, live, organic food approach to eating served humans beautifully. The mental connection to the process of food production enhanced the eating experience, and people were connected to food in an intimate, mindful, and life enhancing way.

Nature's kindness governed whether or not our ancestors would eat. Nature had to provide the rain and sunshine necessary for growing food. This is in direct contrast to the modern experience of going to a supermarket or fast food restaurant, buying whatever we feel like eating as long as we have the money. When nature was honored by our ancestors for providing the food in the form of many earth-based spiritual practices, humans experienced a direct connection between the food harvest and the deity of worship. The gods provided people food, and in gratitude they offered food back to the gods and goddesses of Nature.

With the mass movement of people from the land to cities, food lost its special place and was replaced with fascination for artificial, synthetic, and technologically produced forms of food. No longer was it necessary to hunt or grow food because now it was delivered from short or long distances to nearby markets, and the sacredness of food diminished in proportion to the energy required to obtain it.

How Food and Nonfoods Affect Our Bodies

Over the last thirty years, fast food has penetrated all aspects of American life. From its humble beginnings as hot dog and hamburger stands in southern California[10] convenience foods have spread to every corner of the United States and beyond. Fast food is now served at restaurants and drive-ins, at sporting events, airports, entertainment activities, high schools, elementary schools, and universities, on cruise ships, trains, and airplanes, at Target, Wal-Mart, gas stations, and even at hospital cafeterias. In 1970, Americans spent about $6 billion on fast food; in 2000, they spent more than $110 billion. Recently, Americans were asked by the Gallup organization about their fast food eating habits. Eight in ten Americans surveyed report eating at fastfood restaurants at least monthly, with almost half saying they eat fast food at least weekly. Only 4 percent say they never eat at fastfood restaurants.[10] Americans now spend more money on fast food than on higher education, personal computers, computer software, or new cars. They spend more on fast food than on movies, books, magazines, newspapers, videos, and recorded music—combined.

Buying fast food has become so routine we forget what real food looks like. Erich Schlosser writes in the classic book Fast Food Nation in almost sensual language what the experience of buying convenience products has become for us:

As we pull open the glass door, feel the rush of cool air, walk in, get on line, study the backlit color photographs above the counter, place your order, hand over a few dollars, watch teenagers in uniforms pushing various buttons, and moments later take hold of a plastic tray full of food wrapped in colored paper and cardboard. The whole experience of buying fast food has become so routine, so thoroughly unexceptional and mundane, that it is now taken for granted, like brushing your teeth or stopping for a red light. It has become a social custom as American as a small, rectangular, handheld, frozen, and reheated apple pie.[10]

Food scientists know that the quality we seek most of all in a food, its flavor, is usually present in a quantity too small to be measured by any easy to understand terms such as ounces or teaspoons.

When food is manufactured, food scientists use fancy equipment like spectrometers, gas chromatographs, and headspace vapor analyzers to provide a detailed analysis of a food's flavor components, detecting chemical aromas in amounts as low as one part per billion. One of the problems with manufactured food like substances is that it becomes difficult to trick human awareness into believing the food is "real." Our noses are so sensitive that we can detect aromas present in quantities of a few parts per trillion—an amount equivalent to 0.000000000003 percent. Complex aromas, like those of coffee or roasted meat, are made up of volatile gases from nearly a thousand different chemicals. The smell of a strawberry arises from the magical interaction of at least 350 different chemicals that are present in minute amounts. The chemical that provides the dominant flavor of bell pepper can be tasted in amounts as low as 0.02 parts per billion; one drop is sufficient to add flavor to five average size swimming pools. When food like substances are manufactured flavor additives are used to mimic the taste of real food. The flavor additive is listed last, or second to last, in a processed food's ingredient label. This means that making a food like substance taste like real food is very economical, and the flavor additives cost less than the packaging. The one exception to this are soft drinks which have a larger amount of flavor additives than most other products. Even then, the flavor in a 12-ounce can of Coke costs about half a cent.

Food like substances have to be colored, too, so they can resemble the real food they are pretending to be. Color additives in processed foods are often found in even smaller amounts than the flavor compounds. Food coloring serves many of the same purposes as lipstick, eye shadow, and mascara—and is often made from the same pigments. Titanium dioxide is one example, and is used in processed candies, frosting, and icing to deliver their bright white color; it is a common ingredient in women's cosmetics; and it is the pigment used in many white oil paints and house paints. Does it bother you that we eat the same "flavoring" that is found in house paint?

At fast food restaurants like Burger King, Wendy's, and McDonald's, coloring agents have been added to many of the soft drinks, salad dressings, cookies, condiments, chicken dishes, and sandwich buns. It happens because food researchers have learned that the color of a food can greatly affect how we perceive its taste. Brightly colored foods frequently seem to taste better than bland-looking foods, even when the flavor compounds are identical. Foods that somehow look off-color often seem to have off tastes. For thousands of years, humans have relied on visual cues to help determine what is edible. The color of fruit suggests whether it is ripe, the color of meat whether it is spoiled. This is why food manufacturers manipulate the food like substances so they can *resemble* what real food looks like; they add aromas to manipulate the food like substances so they can *resemble* what real food smells like.

What are the physical and health consequences of eating food additives like colorants and aromatic additives? The Food and Drug Administration, the US government agency which is responsible for the safety of the food we eat and the medications we ingest does not require flavor companies to disclose the ingredients of their additives, so long as all the chemicals are considered by the agency to be GRAS (Generally Regarded As Safe). This lack of public disclosure allows the companies to maintain the secrecy of their formulas. It also hides the fact that flavor compounds sometimes contain more ingredients than the foods being given their taste. Here is one example of the chemical wizardry at play in the manufacturing of "artificial strawberry flavor" which makes a highly processed food taste like a real strawberry.

What is the impact on our bodies of eating and drinking food like substances instead of real food? There are three types of food like substances, processed, junk, and fake foods. **Processed food** is made from real food that has been put through chemical processes and is filled with chemicals and preservatives. Some examples of processed food include beef jerky, canned tea, jam, hot dogs, and low-or-nonfat yogurt with sugar or sucralose.

Image © YaiSirichai, 2014. Used under license from Shutterstock, Inc.

A Burger King strawberry milk shake, contains the following ingredients: amyl acetate, amyl butyrate, amyl valerate, anethol, anisyl formate, benzyl acetate, benzyl isobutyrate, butyric acid, cinnamyl isobutyrate, cinnamyl valerate, cognac essential oil, diacetyl, dipropyl ketone, ethyl acetate, ethyl amylketone, ethyl butyrate, ethyl cinnamate, ethyl heptanoate, ethyl heptylate, ethyl lactate, ethyl methylphenylglycidate, ethyl nitrate, ethyl propionate, ethyl valerate, heliotropin, hydroxyphenyl-2-butanone (10 percent solution in alcohol), α-ionone, isobutyl anthranilate, isobutyl butyrate, lemon essential oil, maltol, 4-methylacetophenone, methyl anthranilate, methyl benzoate, methyl cinnamate, methyl heptine carbonate, methyl naphthyl ketone, methyl salicylate, mint essential oil, neroli essential oil, nerolin, neryl isobutyrate, orris butter, phenethyl alcohol, rose, rum ether, γ-undecalactone, vanillin, and solvent.[10]

Junk foods have very little food in them. Instead, they are made of highly processed foods, hydrogenated fats, chemicals and preservatives, and include anything made with "refined white flour." Some examples are canned breakfast drinks, sugary cold cereals, doughnuts, drive-through fast foods, and soda (like Coke or Pepsi). **Fake foods** are made primarily of chemicals, and usually contain gums and sugar as fillers. Examples are bacon bits, bottled salad dressing, dehydrated soups, and instant coffee.

Nonfoods and Nutrition

All of these nonfoods have one thing in common; it is harder for our bodies to digest, absorb, and eliminate them than the nutritional value they offer our bodies in return. This poor exchange of calories for nutritional value is like a bad investment offering limited return. This leaves our bodies feeling sluggish and deprived.

Thinking back to our ancestral roots, we know that the ability to preserve food was done naturally using salt, fermentation, and sun drying. These simple practices were sustainable and safe for humans. As food preservation has become more and more complex and secretive, food companies now use nearly 6,000 additives and chemicals. Researchers now believe many of these additives can have a devastating impact on our health.

Additives and preservatives are not always negative. Adding vitamins to bread and milk in the early 1900s helped end diseases of nutritional deficiency like pellagra and rickets. When micronutrients were first added to foods, intentions were good, and lives were saved. Now it seems that ways to cheaply process food and manipulate buyers has replaced the higher goals of better health for Americans. Many additives and preservatives are harmful toxic chemicals. It is not yet understood how harmful these chemicals are. Difficulties exist when studying the impact of additives and preservatives on the human body. Suffice it to say, eating fake food takes us as a species so far away from our historical roots the impact could be far worse than even imagined in the worst-case scenario.

Food and Pleasure: A Balancing Act

Some of our favorite guilty pleasures come in the form of fast and processed food. It is important to remember that it is not necessary to eliminate ALL of the less desirable food choices we make. We all enjoy the occasional cheeseburger, fries, Coke, or potato chips. When we begin to understand the consequences of changing an occasional treat into an everyday event, we can make better choices about how many of these "treats" we are willing to eat.

In order to avoid many of the questionable and possibly deadly additives contained in processed foods, you may wish to make changes in your diet. Here it is helpful to consider an evolutionary (more gradual) approach to change, rather than a revolutionary (cutting everything out at once) way of changing. If you are interested in making small changes to improve your overall diet and possibly your health, try these ten steps to move in the right direction. It may be helpful to consider one of these changes a month.

1. As a general rule, if there are five or more ingredients on a label, or if you don't recognize or can't pronounce the words, don't buy it or eat it! Instead, choose the real thing.
2. Avoid products containing
   a. nitrates and nitrites (including sodium nitrite)
   b. sulfites (including metabisulfites)
   c. sulfur dioxide
   d. benzoic acid (aka sodium benzoate)
   e. BHT (butylated hydroxytoluene)
   f. BHA (butylated hydroxyanisole)
   g. coloring
   h. coal tar
   i. propylene glycol
   j. MSG (monosodium glutamate)
   k. refined or bleached flour (i. e., whitened using chloride oxide)
3. Don't eat partially hydrogenated or hydrogenated trans fats.
4. Don't eat products containing sugar substitutes such as aspartame, sucralose, saccharine, or stevia.
5. Avoid products with a long shelf life—the longer they can last on a shelf, the worse they are for your body.
6. Minimize your consumption of enriched products. All vitality has been removed from them during processing.
7. Avoid GMO foods. Nearly all processed food contains GMOs.
8. Avoid products made with ingredients such as "natural flavoring" or "natural coloring."
9. Avoid products with added sugar. New recommendations from the World Health Organization (WHO) state that added sugars should be limited to 20 grams per day[11] (equivalent of 6 teaspoons of sugar). For reference, a 12 ounce can of Coke has 10 teaspoons of added sugar, a Yoplait original yogurt has nearly 7 teaspoons of added sugar—2.7 times more sugar than a Krispy Kreme doughnut!
10. Choose mostly whole fresh foods—fruits and vegetables, the brighter colors the better and make real food the centerpiece of your diet. Think of a dinner plate—fill half with fresh fruits and vegetables, ¼ with lean protein, and the other ¼ with whole grains like brown rice, sweet potatoes, legumes, or whole grain bread.

Begin to notice how you feel as you eliminate processed food from your diet. Notice your improved digestion, lack of mood swings, staying fuller longer, better energy, and less mental fog. You are on your way to optimizing your health, making an investment in your body's future, and feeling better.

Food as Sacred—Food IS Sacred

Throughout human history, particularly in native cultures, food was known as sacred. The word *sacred* is not a religious term but rather one that simply means "set apart" or not of the ordinary.[12] It is also related to *sacrifice*. This may mean that something is sacred because it came from something sacrificed. For example, we speak of military cemeteries and famous battlefields as sacred. In ancient times, some temples, mountains, or forests were sacred because animals were sacrificed to a god in those places. All food is sacred in the sense that the life of a plant or animal has been sacrificed to feed another being.

The opposite of the sacred, of course, is the profane. Something in our ancient memory understands that as we consume mindlessly manufactured and technologically tortured so-called food we lose connection to the specialness of food and its origins. This in turn makes it more likely we will think twice about eating processed, genetically modified, and chemically laden foods that have been produced using massive amounts of resources and ecological compromise.[12] We begin to recognize the cost to our physiology and our health that consuming food like substances renders; we begin to recognize the cost to our souls that this practice engenders.

Image © NataliTerr, 2014. Used under license from Shutterstock, Inc.

Who do we worship now, or thank for the bounty found in the supermarket? Our experience of acquiring food in our times is stripped of all gratitude and ritual. Instead, we expect food to be there whatever we want, whenever we want it. We eat out of season, and expect strawberries in the winter, even if they come from South America. Instead of carefully choosing from Earth's bounty, we purchase processed food products that are shallow stand-ins for the plants that provided the basic ingredients. It is this loss of connection to food that leads to mindless eating done out of habit and without awareness. Reconnecting to food and its sacredness mean reconnecting with ourselves.

How can we begin to reconnect to the sanctity of food and in so doing increase our emotional nourishment? The writer Peter Bolland suggests in "The Sacrament of Food," the most sacred space in our homes is not the yoga room, or the altar with the candle, or the chair by the window where we meditate and pray. "Maybe the most sacred room in your house is the kitchen."[13] Our relationship with food begins far in advance of preparing it in the kitchen. Here are some suggestions for cultivating a more mindful relationship with the food we eat:

1. Know where your food comes from. Read labels, ask questions, and research sources for whole, organic foods where you live.
2. Consider becoming a community supported agriculture (CSA) member. This allows you to buy directly from the farmer or grower.
3. Give thanks when you shop—thank the food you purchase, thank market staff, and give thanks that you can afford to shop.

4. Commit to purchasing 10 percent or more of food that is grown locally.
5. Practice mindful meal planning. Plan strategies for eating in places where nourishing food is served or plan to bring healthy snacks with you.
6. Take a moment or two to stop before eating and give thanks for your food. Remember to thank the people who grew, harvested, transported, and distributed your food. Thank plants and animals for their lives and the sacrifice they made with their lives so that you can be fed.
7. Regularly enjoy food with family and friends. Cook and eat meals together. Share the blessings of food with each other in potlucks or other gatherings.
8. Occasionally share extra food or leftovers with neighbors or people who are not in your family or circle of friends. Sharing food with others communicates a subtle message that you are concerned about their well-being in hard times. Reaching out in this way encourages connection to others around food so that when someone has little or no food, others are more motivated to share.

Image © Andresr, 2014. Used under license from Shutterstock, Inc.

Intelligent Shopping (From the Supermarket to the Dinner Table)

"Researchers have shown that what we eat doesn't depend solely on signals sent by the brain to maintain a stable weight. Another region of the brain, with different circuitry, is also involved, and often it's in charge. This is known as the reward system. And in America, in the fight between energy balance and reward, the reward system is winning."

—Dr. David Kessler, "The End of Overeating: Taking Control of the Insatiable American Appetite"[14]

Sustainable living and conscious eating is about limiting waste, especially when it comes to purchasing and using food. Wasting food is expensive, and can especially add up throughout the year. Rather than "cleaning everything off your plate," think about buying, cooking, and storing foods properly. Now is a great time to start changing "food waste behaviors."

The first rule in stopping food waste is to be a smart shopper. Start out by going through your cabinets, fridge, and freezer and make note of what you already have. Then it's time to be creative and develop a meal plan to use all those ingredients. Make sure you are reading your expiration dates correctly. McKinsey reports that misreading expiration dates accounts for around 20 percent of all food waste,[15] so look carefully at expiration dates. A great tool to help your overall meal planning is ReadySetEat.com, where you can enter the ingredients you have and a list of recipes will be displayed. Make sure that you only prepare enough for each meal and any guests—don't over prepare!

Another tip to remember is that, while most of us buy about 80 percent of the same foods every week, you can use your register receipt as your shopping list. Mark off what you already have, and leave room at the bottom to write any additional items you may need to make this week's recipes. Now, you're off to the supermarket!

With over 34,000 supermarkets in the US, there are more than 30,000 food products filling the shelves.[16] Supermarkets offer endless aisles of food choices, and wholesale stares encourage us to consume in bulk to save money. The key to intelligent supermarket shopping is developing a clear game plan that encourages you to buy only what food you and your family needs.

The time of day you go shopping makes a difference, too. Brian Wansink, director of the Food and Brand Lab at Cornell University, has found the time of day you shop can make a difference as well. If you shop between 1 p.m. and 3 p.m. there is a tendency to buy less food and healthier foods than when it is closer to dinnertime, between 3 p.m. and 5 p.m.[17] so as the saying goes, never go shopping when you are hungry.

We know the basics of supermarket shopping. the outside perimeter of the store layout has healthful foods like fresh fruits and vegetables, dairy products, animal protein products. Inside the perimeter and organized in ways that encourage you to spend more on less healthy foods are snacks, soda, fruit juices, alcohol, and other processed food products. In addition to spending most of your time in the outside perimeter of the store, here are some other suggestions to help you navigate the grocery isles:

1. Plan ahead

  a. Always shop with a list. Write down your shopping list. It helps you stay focused while strolling the aisles.
  b. Post your shopping list on the refrigerator and add to it as you need to replenish your food and household items. This saves time when you are ready to shop.

2. Review your list

  a. Before heading out to the store, use the shopping circular to help plan the major meals for the week. After planning your menu, check your pantry and fridge to take inventory of what you need.
  b. Always add a variety of fresh fruits and vegetables for side dishes and snacks.
  c. Include a few treats to avoid feeling deprived.
  d. Do not forget the staples: milk, eggs, juice, cereal, bread, and yogurt. These basic food items are a good place to reduce fat and calories because you can choose low-fat or nonfat versions of most of these items. Some of these items also help increase daily fiber intake.

3. Shopping strategy

  a. Get through the supermarket quickly by organizing your list according to the store layout. Most supermarkets are similarly designed, with perishable foods, such as fruits, vegetables, meats, dairy, eggs, and breads around the perimeter of the store, and aisles and end-displays containing cleaning and paper products, health and beauty aids, packaged and canned goods, and frozen foods.

b. Purchase only the items on your shopping list. Resist impulse purchases that tend to be high fat and high calorie. Allow yourself only three impulse items and write them down as you buy them, that way you will feel satisfied and still stay on budget.

c. Eat before you shop. Never go to the supermarket with an empty stomach. You are likely to end up with more food than you need and more fattening selections.

d. Back in the kitchen; use a trick from the Food and Brand Lab based on what is called The Delboeuf Illusion, which recommends the use of smaller plates to serve. Research at Cornell has shown that we tend to put more food on larger plates, which often leads to more food being uneaten and wasted.[17]

Where Does Your Food Come From?— the Industrialization of the American Diet

"Is it just a coincidence that as the portion of our income spent on food has declined, spending on health care has soared? In 1960 Americans spent 17.5 percent of their income on food and 5.2 percent . . . on health care. Since then, those numbers have flipped: Spending on food has fallen to 9.9 percent, while spending on health care has climbed to 16 percent of national income."

—Michael Pollan, In Defense of Food

We've learned in this chapter about the changing American diet, and how our meals are made up more often by processed foods, stripped of their original ingredients, and filled with added nonfood ingredients. More often than not, this ingredient is sugar, specifically fructose. According to Pollan per capita fructose consumption has increased 25 percent in the past thirty years. The mass production of food for a mass society was of course inevitable, but was it also inevitable, as one nutrition expert put it, that its placed us in the middle of a national experiment in the overconsumption of glucose, the form in which fructose is metabolized in the liver and transmitted by insulin to the cells to be used as energy. Scientists now know that glucose metabolism leads to fat deposition in the body[18] changing the way the body uses glucose as

an adaptation to this industrialized form of sugar. We assimilate the complex nutrients of traditional foods slowly, but the rush of refined sugars supplied by our industrialized diet overwhelms the ability of the protein hormone insulin to process it. The result is a sudden jolt of energy and soon a craving for more, as the unused glucose is stored as triglycerides, that is, fat. "An American born in 2000 has a 1 in 3 chance of developing diabetes in his lifetime," Pollan writes. "80 percent of diabetics will suffer from heart disease." Pollan suggest that there is a global pandemic in the making which leads only to a global pandemic of solutions in the form of diabetes and kidney medications. It is almost as if the industrialization of food has led to the industrialization of health care. All in all, whether one examines this on an agricultural or a biological level, it is unsustainable.

This industrialization of the food system is supported through an elaborately designed food production process that manufactures this new "food" that many Americans eat. Factory farms have replaced traditional farms, with one of the largest cash crops being beef. The industrialization of the food supply is, of course, part of the process of industrialization itself, but it dangerously transformed food in the mid-1970s when in response to rapidly rising food prices many unhappy consumers protested and were heard by the highest levels of the American government. Under the Nixon administration, a cheap and ambitious food policy was adopted which was solely designed to produce and sell large quantities of calories as cheaply as possible. This made exporting affordable food overseas possible as well as producing very cheap food domestically. The American government has provided federal funds to subsidize farmers since the 1930s but it was usually designed to encourage farmers to limit production in order to maintain stable prices. Under this new subsidy formula, farmers were encouraged to plant crops like corn, soy, and wheat in giant quantities, driving production up and prices down.

With farmers maximizing production, the big players in industrialized farming got into the business of food production, changing the face of American farming forever. Enter corporations like Monsanto, Cargill, Archer Daniels Midland, and General Mills. These corporations bought up small farms, creating gigantic factory farms. The types of foods produced by these farms change and overall American farmers and American farming corporations now produce an average of 600 more calories per person per day, and the price of food has fallen. This has changed the way we eat, and we now eat at least 300 more calories a day than we consumed in 1985.[19] Almost 25 percent of these additional calories come from added sugars, particularly fructose, another quarter from added fat (in the form of soybean oil), and the other 50 percent from added grains (mostly refined). These additional calories supply lots of energy (calories) but since they are so highly refined, they supply little else. Instead of the intelligent digestive design we described earlier in this chapter, these industrialized nonfood calories become excess fat.[20]

With gigantic corporations in the food business, it was easy to find a way to use all of the extra corn, soybeans, and wheat. The new cash crop of beef was born, and giant feedlots (called CAFO's—consolidated animal feeding operations) were created to produce extralarge cattle. With cattle moved into feedlots, a nontraditional way of raising beef was born, and the diet of cows changed from grazing on grasses to corn. With cows eating nontraditional diets of corn farmers are able to pack in thousands of additional calories making bigger and bigger cows which are also fatter than their grassfed counter-

Image © Bernhard Richter, 2014. Used under license from Shutterstock, Inc.

parts. However, cows are jammed together in giant feedlots, and the new diet of corn and soybeans creates health problems. Since cows are not adapted to eat and digest corn or soybeans, they develop digestive issues, which are treated through antibiotics and other medications. This entire process of the mass production of our beef is unseen by most Americans, which is fortunate for the food industry. Michael Pollan writes that if we could see where our beef comes from (and chicken and pork), it would transform the way we eat overnight. A consequence of this hidden production of our food supply is the inability

Image © Graphic Compressor, 2014. Used under license from Shutterstock, Inc.

to witness the industrialized way the animals used for our food are maintained in shockingly inhumane conditions and brutally sacrificed for our food.

Pollan reminds us in *The Omnivore's Dilemma* (27) that no other country raises and slaughters its food animals quite as intensively or as brutally as we do. We have removed ourselves from the animals we eat. If we could see the way we raise and kill our animals, he believes that this transparency would lead to the ending of how we raise, kill, and eat animals the way we do. "Tail docking and sow crates and beak clipping would disappear overnight, and the days of slaughtering four hundred heads of cattle an hour would promptly come to an end—for who could stand the sight?"[21] This would of course make meat more expensive, but the benefit would be the probability we'd eat a lot less of it. If this were to happen, it would allow us to eat animals with "consciousness, ceremony, and respect they deserve"[22] thus bringing us back into harmony with our food.

What about GMOs?

Another consequence of the industrialization of food is the birth of genetically modified organisms (GMOs). They are organisms in which the genetic material (DNA) has been altered in a way that does not occur naturally. The technology is often called "modern biotechnology" or "gene technology," sometimes also "recombinant DNA technology" or "genetic engineering." It allows selected individual genes to be transferred from one organism into another, also between nonrelated species. GMOs most commonly refer to crop or plants created for human or animal consumption.[23]

GMOs have created a great deal of controversy in the US and abroad, particularly in Europe. Consumers, environmental activists, scientists, and government officials have all raised concerns regarding the nature and safety of GMOs in relation to any benefits they may have. Of particular concern is whether or not adequate research has been conducted to determine whether GMOs are safe for long-term use. Other concerns include whether the laws governing biotechnology are outdated and lack regulatory oversight.[24] Adding to the confusion in the United States is sheer number of governing agencies involved in regulation. Currently, there are three different agencies governing biotechnology and genetic engineering. The EPA evaluates GM plants for environmental safety, the USDA evaluates whether the plant is safe to grow, and the FDA evaluates whether the plant is safe to eat.[25] Consumers are also concerned over the lack of transparency of GM food products in processed foods. At this time, the FDA does not require labeling of GM products, nor do they require premarket safety testing of GM foods.[26]

Typical GM Foods in the American Food System

The following is a list of GE foods that have been approved for commercial use[27]:

Alfalfa	Potato
Cherry Tomato	Rapeseed (Canola)
Chicory (Cichorium intybus)	Rice
Corn	Soybean
Cotton	Squash
Flax	Sugarbeet
Papaya	Tomatoes

The two most common concerns regarding GM foods are the potential for allergenicity, and antibiotic resistance.[28] Allergenicity is the transfer of a new gene into a plant and subsequent creation of a novel protein may create a new allergen or cause an allergic reaction in susceptible individuals. For example, an allergenic Brazil-nut gene was transformed into a transgenic soybean variety, resulting in allergic reactions to the GE product.[28]

Antibiotics resistance markers have been used to verify successful gene transfer in organisms. Bacteria in the gut, thus giving antibiotic resistance to the bacteria, may take up the antibiotic resistance gene. This can potentially lead to disease-causing bacteria becoming untreatable using current antibiotics, leading to increased spread of infections, and diseases in the human population.[29] Currently, marker genes that avoid medical or environmental hazards are now replacing antibiotic resistance markers.[30]

The issue of GMOs is complex. For each application of biotechnology exists differing purposes, methodologies, and outcomes of potential risks and benefits. More research regarding the environmental, economical, and medical impacts are encouraged in order to find recommendations that make sense. Due to this complexity, judgment of whether or not you should consume GM foods should be made on a case-by-case basis. Making a personal assessment of the risks and benefits is recommended. For those wishing to avoid GM foods, a whole-foods diet is the best approach.

Mindful Eating—an Ancient Practice for Modern Problems[31]

Have you ever finished a cookie and wanted to have just one more bite? Are you surprised when you eat your way through a bag of chips or a box of crackers? Do feelings of "overfull" and "stuffed" hit your awareness after you eat?

If any of this is true for you, you're not alone. Our fast paced lives discourage mindful eating, which requires tuning in, paying attention, and staying centered. Many of us eat watching TV, while driving, or working. Often, we eat while talking on the telephone or surfing the Internet. In the rush to get things done, fast eating, filling one forkful after another and swallowing food without tasting becomes the norm. Fullness is subtle, and sometimes quickly moving through meals leads to missed signals the body sends to the brain. Overeating becomes unconscious; far past "enough"; it happens again in the next meal. Struggling with weight, we wonder what we're so hungry for. Experts say that it is not only important what we eat, but, how we eat. By paying attention and making the choice to eat "mindfully," through practice the experience of how to be fully satisfied by food without overeating becomes realized.

Mindful eating encourages awareness through the entire experience of eating, including selecting and preparing food. When eating mindfully, food is chosen that is both pleasing and nourishing to the body. Using all of the senses to taste, savor, and enjoy food, eating is pleasurable. This process of deliberately paying attention without judgment allows freedom from reactive, habitual patterns of thinking, feeling, and acting which often include harsh and unkind statements towards ourselves.

Mindful eating is about making peace with food, and eating according to body needs. When we eat mindfully, we eat to support the body's naturally healthy state, inviting balance, choice, wisdom, and acceptance. Being in the moment and paying attention while we eat allows us to slow down, chew well, taste thoroughly, and enjoy eating. Different than a "diet," mindful eating does not rely on weighing or measuring food, restricting or avoiding certain foods, labeling some foods "good" and others "bad" or counting fat grams or calories. Eating mindfully and encouraging self-acceptance allows us to be free from worrying about body size or "ideal" body weight. Instead, the practice of mindful eating encourages the following principles:

1. **Eat when hungry**. Watch for the body's hunger cues as a signal that it is time to eat. Eat enough to feel satisfied and comfortably full, not stuffed. For most of us, practicing mindful eating means having several small meals throughout the day and one or two planned snacks. Whole foods, mostly plant-based meals including fresh fruits, vegetables, legumes, whole grains, and lean protein promotes satiety and mealtime satisfaction.

2. **Eat in a distraction free zone.** Pay attention to how food tastes, and what feelings arise while eating. Take five or six slow deep breaths when sitting down to eat. Many people benefit from saying silent grace or what mindful practitioners call a food blessing before beginning meals. No matter which approach is chosen, taking the time to slow down and savor food begins the practice of mindfulness where the possibility of change begins.

3. **Eat what is desired**. Overeating out of deprivation often happens when eating what "should" be eaten instead of what is desired. Labeling certain foods "bad" and restricting food may also lead to searching for food whether hungry or not. Eat rich, satisfying foods in smaller amounts, savoring every bite.

4. **Eat until satisfied, not uncomfortable**. It takes about twenty minutes for the brain to register fullness while eating. Slow down, pay attention, and stop before feeling stuffed. Practice putting down the fork in between bites, and take a breath or two to keep relaxed and aware while eating. Wait a bit, and if still hungry, have more. Consistently eating until stuffed means not listening to the bodies' signal of fullness. Occasionally overeating is normal. To change habitual overeating, paying attention allows the possibility of change. Noticing patterns provides the opportunity to choose a different outcome.

Image © Phil Jones, 2014. Used under license from Shutterstock, Inc.

5. **Use the Healthy Eating Plate Model as a guide**. This tool helps develop trust for cues of satisfaction and fullness. Using the Healthy Plate provides freedom from weighing, measuring, or counting calories. Fill ½ the plate with vegetables, ¼ with lean protein, and ¼ with whole grains like rice, potatoes, pasta, or fresh fruit. This eating approach helps reduce anxiety of how much food is enough or too much. Building mealtime servings with delicious foods in appropriate portions allows healthful eating in exactly the right amounts and the right choices.

Remember that food is pleasure, and should be enjoyed. Using sight, smell, and taste while eating allows all of the senses to participate in the enjoyment of a delicious and nourishing meal. This mindful approach incorporating sensory stimuli encourages eating satisfaction and effortless weight management. Be patient—remember it is called a "practice"—not "perfection"—since it takes time and attention to create a different outcome. The body moves to the weight it is supposed to be, supported through the practice of mindfulness.

References

1. Cousens, G., *Conscious Eating*. Berkeley, CA: North Atlantic Books, 2000.

2. Lair, C., *Feeding the Whole Family*. Seattle, WA: Sasquatch Books, 2008.

3. Alberts, Bruce, Johnson, Alexander, & Lewis, Johnson, Raiff, Martin, Roberts, Keith, & Walter, Peter, "Energy Conversion: Mitochondria and Chloroplasts." In *Molecular Biology of the Cell*, 4th ed. New York: Garland Science, 2002.

4. Fahy, E., Subramaniam, S., Muphy, R., Nishijima, M., Raetz, C., Shimizu, T., Spencer, F., Van Meer, G., Wakelam, M., & Dennis, E. A., "Update of the LIPID MAPS Comprehensive Classification System for Lipids," *Journal of Lipid Research* 50 (Supplement) (2009): S9–S14. doi:10.1194/jlr. R800095-JLR200.

5. Fulkerson, L., Wendel, B., Corry, J., Campbell, T. C., Esselstyn, C. B., Balcazar, R., Monica Beach Media (Firm), & Virgil Films (Firm), *Forks over knives*. Santa Monica, CA: Monica Beach Media, 2011.

6. Division of Nutrition, Physical Activity, and Obesity, *Overweight and Obesity*. The Centers for Disease Control and Prevention, 2014. www.cdc.gov/ovesity/data/adult.html.

7. Micozzi, M., "Nutrition and Hydration." In *Fundamentals of Complementary and Alternative Medicine*, 4th ed. St. Louis, MO: Elsevier, 2011.

8. Bente, L. & Gerrior, S. A., "Selected food highlights of the 20th Century: U. S. Food Supply Series," *Family Economics and Nutrition Review* 14 (2002): 43–52.

9. Gardner, M., Wansink, B., Kim, J., & Park, S., "Better Moods for Better Eating?: How Mood Influences Food Choice," *Journal of Consumer Psychology* (2014). doi:http://dx.doi.org/10.1016/j.jcps.2014.01.002.

10. Schlosser, E., *Fast Food Nation: The Dark Side of the All-American Meal*. Boston: Houghton Mifflin, 2001.

11. World Health Organization, *WHO Opens Public Consultation on Draft Sugars Guideline*, 2014. www.who.int/mediacentre/news/notes/2014/consultation-sugar-guideline/en.

12. Ikerd, J., *Reclaiming the Sacred in Food and Farming*. University of Missouri, 2002. web.missouri.edu/~ikerdj/papers/Sacred.html.

13. Bolland, P., "Ten Truths from the Kitchen." In *Thinking Through: Philosophy, Mythology, Spirituality and Transformational Wisdom*. peterbolland.blogspot.com/2012/07/ten-truths-from-kitchen.html.

14. Oliver, M., *Beans Green and Yellow. From Swan: Poems and Prose Poems*. Boston: Beacon Press, 2010.

15. National Resources Defense Council. *Wasted: How America Is Losing Up to 40 percent of its Food from Farm to Fork to Landfill*. NRDC Issue Paper. IP:12-06-B, 2012.

16. Tropp, D., Ragland, E., & Barham, J., *Supply Chain Basics: The Dynamics of Change in the U. S. Food Marketing Environment*. U. S. Department of Agriculture. Washington DC: Agricultural Marketing Service Marketing Services Program, 2008.

17. Wansink, B., *Mindless Eating*. New York, NY: Bantam Dell, 2006.

18. Wilcox, G., "Insulin and Insulin Resistance," *The Clinical Biochemist Reviews* 26 no. 2 (2005): 19–39.

19. USDA, *Changes in Eating Patterns and Diet Quality Among Working Age Adults*. United States Department of Agriculture, 2014.

20. Taubes, G., "What Makes You Fat: Too Many Calories, or the Wrong Carbohydrates?" *Scientific American Volume* 39 no. 3 (2013).

21. Pollan, M., *The Omnivore's Dilemma*. New York, NY: Penguin Books, 2006.

22. Southgate, C., *The Groaning of Creation: God, Evolution and the Problem of Evil*. Louisville, KY: Westminster John Knox Press, 2008.

23. World Health Organization, *20 Questions on Genetically Modified Foods*. 2014. Accessed March 30, http://www.who.int/foodsafety/publications/biotech/20questions/en.

24. Whitman, D., *Genetically Modified Foods: Harmful or Helpful?* CSA Discovery Guides, April 2000.

25. Pretty, J., "The Rapid Emergence of Genetic Modification in World Agriculture: Contested Risks and Benefits," *Environmental Conservation* 28 no. 3 (2001): 248–62.

26. Kimbrell, A., "The Hidden Health Hazards of Genetically Engineered Foods," *Food Safety Review*: Center for Food Safety, 2000.

27. Grace Communications, *Genetic Engineering*. New York, NY: Grace Communications foundation, 2014. Accessed March 30, 2014, http://www. sustainabletable. org/264/genetic-engineering.

28. Nordlee, J. A., Taylor, S. L., Townsend, J. A., Thomas, L. A., & Bush, R. K. "Identification of a Brazil-nut Allergen in Transgenic Soybeans," *New England Journal of Medicine* 334 no. 11 (1996): 688–92.

29. GMO Compass, *Antibiotic Resistance Genes: A threat?* 2014. Accessed March 30, 2014, http://www.gmo-compass.org/eng/safety/human_health/46.antibioitc_resistance_genes_threat.html.

30. Read, D., *Use of Antibiotic Resistance Marker Genes in Genetically Modified Organisms*. ERMA New Zealand, 2000. Accessed March 30, 2014, http://www.epa.govt.nz/publications/pp-er-gi-01-1-pdf.pdf.

31. Schmidt, L. & Morrow, K., *Mindful Eating: Using Attention and Awareness to Satisfy Hunger*. Seattle, WA: Northwest Prime Time, 2012.

QUIZ QUESTIONS

1. T/F:Eating foods that are appropriate to our own individual needs extracts energy from the environment in harmony with the natural world.

_____

_____

_____

_____

2. The consequences for eating in connection with the world around us include:
   a. eating mindfully
   b. eating consciously
   c. losing weight
   d. a & b only
   e. all of the above

3. T/F: the body's ability to adapt in the face of changing conditions is possible because of the principle of self-regulation.

_____

_____

_____

_____

4. T/F: Mitochondria are called our "cellular power plants" because they generate most of the cell's supply of ATP.

_____

_____

_____

_____

5. Lipids perform major functions in the body, including:
   a. storing energy
   b. signaling
   c. structural support
   d. all of the above

6. T/F: Protein converts readily into energy, and has a big role in providing fuel to the body.

_____

_____

_____

_____

7. T/F: Our hunter gatherer ancestors were unable to eat regularly, so they developed a special appreciation for food.

_____

_____

_____

_____

8. The things that contributed to our losing appreciation for our food include:
   a. moving from the land to the cities
   b. supermarkets
   c. eating whatever we want, regardless of the season
   d. food available everywhere, even at gas stations
   e. all of the above

9. Mindful eating means all EXCEPT:
   a. making peace with food
   b. paying attention to the entire eating experience without judgment
   c. being mindful when choosing and preparing food
   d. eating as much as you want
   e. eating whatever you desire, with attention

10. T/F:In order to lose weight, it can be helpful to learn your own signals of hunger and fullness.

_____

_____

_____

_____

MINDFUL AWARENESS REFLECTION JOURNAL

4 Step MAC Guide

Choose one mindful experience as you begin your reflection.

Empathically Acknowledge

Describe your experience

_____

_____

_____

Intentional Attention

Describe what you noticed

Breath
Body
Emotions
Thoughts
Senses

Accept Without Judgment

Describe judgment; acceptance

_____

_____

_____

Willingly Choose

Intention/willingness; new perspective

_____

_____

_____

Mindful Mac Meditation

Describe your meditation experiences. What did you learn?

_____

_____

_____

Name: _____   Date: _____

CHAPTER CRITICAL THINKING AND ACTIVITY JOURNAL

This is an opportunity for you to fully describe your thoughts, opinions and experience following the reading and activities.

The most important information/key concepts we need to understand from these chapters are:

_____

_____

_____

_____

How can I use the information in the chapters to help me with my daily mindfulness practice?

_____

_____

_____

_____

In what ways will the material learned in these chapters help me manage my stress more effectively?

_____

_____

_____

_____

What are your thoughts and feedback regarding the information and activities for each chapter?

_____

_____

_____

_____

CHAPTER FIVE

IMPACT OF GLOBAL ENVIRONMENTAL STRESS ON UNIVERSAL WELL-BEING

Be the Solution

By Pat Duryea

Photograph: courtesy of Maria Napoli

"I yearn to taste clean spring water,
My body heals with food grown in mineral-based soil
My lungs expand joyfully breathing clean air
I deserve no less
Neither do you"

Maria Napoli

Abraham Maslow, in the early 1950s, delineated a five-stage pyramid model of individual needs. At the bottom of this pyramid are the basic needs of air, food, and water. Maslow always contended that all individuals have an innate desire to move up the hierarchy of needs toward self-actualization.[1]

Merriam-Webster defines self-actualization as "to realize fully one's potential." *Merriam-Webster* also defines well-being as "the state of being happy, healthy, or successful (realizing one's potential)."[2] Thus the author interchanges these two words for a simplification of understanding to mean that every person has an innate desire to live in a state of well-being.

This state of well-being is measured in as many different ways as there are people, but if we were to look at humanity as a whole, made up of mothers, fathers, and children all around the world, we would find an elemental desire in all of us. A desire for food, water, and a place to live in happiness.

A 2012 report prepared by the World Economic Forum Global Agenda Council on Well-being and Global Success took seriously the idea of "if you treasure it, measure it."[3] Through different surveys and indexes they measured the well-being of schools, companies, and communities around the world. The report delineated three ways in which our well-being enables us to perform better at home, school, work, and in our communities. The identified measures were:

1. The productivity of workers and the profitability of the companies they work for increased as individual well-being improved
2. Resilient families and stronger children come from individuals with high levels of well-being
3. Individuals with high well-being are greater contributing members of their communities.[3]

Over 2,500 years ago it was known that where a person lives impacts the stress and well-being of the person. Hippocrates, according to Lloyd, in the Well-being and Global Success report stated "as a general rule that people's habits follow the nature of the land where they live."[3,4,5] Habits that we will conclude often lead to stressors on our universal well-being.

Another global analysis of 150 countries concluded that there are five universal, interconnected elements that shape our lives. The five elements include financial, physical, community, social, and career elements.[5]

Even though it takes all five of these elements for individuals to experience an overall sense of well-being the two elements of physical and community well-being are most relevant to this chapter. Physical well-being is attributed to having enough health and energy each day to get all the things done that one wants to accomplish. Energy comes from consuming daily nutritious food from healthy soil—and, community well-being that includes the human engagement in the community where one lives and feeling secure about the air one breathes and the water one drinks.

Taking the physical and community components of the five essential elements and Maslow's human desire for well-being, let us take a look at how we progress toward this state of well-being—and, more importantly, how this progress is often thwarted by complex societal issues such as soil, water, and air pollution, on a global level.

"Approximately 40 percent of deaths worldwide are caused by water, air, and soil pollution due to environmental degradation and growth in world population, which contribute to an increase in human disease."[6] This environmental degradation, or global stress plays mayhem on our universal well-being. This chapter will describe how each and every one of us can be a solution toward overcoming this stress instead of being a part of the overall problem.

How Did We Get Here?

How did we get to where we are with a worldwide accumulation of pollution that causes such a state of stress on our global well-being? Some 40,000 years ago man discovered how to "change the patterns of nature," the evolution from living in the forests where nature created its own form of population control to the Agricultural Revolution that gained momentum approximately 10,000 years ago when humans learned to grow food and herd animals.[7]

As people began to grow their own food and herd animals they started to grow roots and created small settlements. A natural result of this type of domestication came more and more people. Astonishingly, in the ninth century the world population grew from a few million to over a quarter of a billion people—with the discoveries of coal and then oil, life was flourishing and so was the population. What took over 200,000 years to reach—the first billion people, took only 130 years to double.[7]

As there were many new discoveries of tools and technologies to improve their lives, the world population grew annually until in our world today we have over 7 billion people.[8] With this exponential growth in population came many complex societal issues including pollution of the soil, water, and air. Societal issues that added major stress to the overall well-being of the world. Let us take a look at each of these issues separately for a moment.

What Happened to Our SOIL?

Image © romrf, 2014. Used under license from Shutterstock, Inc.

First, let us discuss what soil is. Many of us would simply say it is something in which to grow plants. A farmer might suggest that it is the foundation from which plants get their nutrients and water—but, a pedologist, or soil scientist, would exclaim that there are over 40 different soil groups around the world such as Chernozem, tropical, desert, and tundra, each with its own profile affected by erosion, agriculture, weather changes, etc.[9] A plethora of information exists regarding soil and its properties, but most is far beyond the scope of this chapter. Let it suffice to say that most soils are mixtures of silt, sand, and clay with some organic materials mixed which is in a constant process of evolution in which we grow our crops for food. The most important fact to remember about soil, according to Kellogg, is that it deeply influences the life of man.[9]

Before farming, hunter-gatherers roamed the land and ate the food that they discovered—when their food stuffs ran out, they moved on to another location and started all over. One day a brilliant woman thought—what if we take the seeds from wheat and barley and put them back into the earth. Whaala . . . the beginning of farming and a whole new lifestyle!

Over the centuries, there was not only a massive increase in agricultural productivity but farm technology became a new field of study.[10] With these new discoveries came an increase in crop yield. Crop yield quickly became the gold standard—however, over many years this new drive for increase in crop yield lead to not only the usage of commercial fertilizers but a depletion of soil minerals—minerals that took millions of years to be created through earth shifts that pulverized rocks, decaying plant life in the forests, and animal waste products—minerals that cannot be replaced overnight by commercial fertilizer companies.

A landmark study done at the University of Texas, studied nutritional data from both 1950 and 1999 for over 40 fruits and vegetables. The discovery indicated declines in the amount of protein, calcium, phosphorus, iron, riboflavin, and vitamin C over the past 50 years. According to this team, the declining nutritional content of these fruits and vegetables can be chalked up to the preponderance of agricultural practices in the United States.[11]

Not only in America is the soil no longer providing plants with the mineral elements which are so essential to human nourishment and nutritional health, but all around the world. Let us look at one continent where the population continues to grow at higher rates than any other continent—Africa. In Africa, where over 65 percent of the people depend on agriculture for their livelihood, population pressure on

land resources forces farmers to use marginal land areas to grow their food. Shockingly, 96 percent of the countries in Africa show an annual negative balance of nutrients.[12]

In third world countries, such as Africa, crop yield is a thought furthermost from many farmers' minds. Growing food, and lots of it, is the most important thought for farmers feeding an ever growing population. Using the same fields to grow the same crops year after year also depletes the minerals. With a depletion of the minerals from the world's soil the quality of the foods that we are able to grow has diminished. Many people are eating more and more food and ingesting less and less nutrients.

As our world continues to fight over soil, the search for alternative fuels has led to the practice of monocropping.[13] In countries like Brazil, monocropping of sugarcane has become very popular as our dependence on agrofuels becomes greater. Large areas of land are set aside and utilized by governmental programs such as Proalcool for the commercialization and export of the sugar-alcohol (ethanol) complex—not only does monocropping deplete the soils of its nutrients but it uses the best agricultural lands for this industry robbing the people of Brazil and other countries of food producing fields. Besides the depletion of the nutrients from our soils there are specific contaminants such as arsenic, mercury, cadmium, polycyclic aromatic hydrocarbons (PAH's), hexachlorobenzene, metal pollutants creating by industries and

dumped into our water sources which flows into our soil. According to 2007 estimates, soil contamination requiring clean up in Europe alone is approximately 250,000 sites.[14] Suffice it to say common sense would tell us that our soils have been depleted of its nutrients and contaminated by an excess of chemicals, many of which are carcinogenic. Currently, our soil can be considered detrimental to the health of humanity . . . and, thus our global well-being.

Below is a list of practical solutions for how you can protect our soil.

Unless you are a farmer or plant a garden for your home use, thinking about soil is probably the last thought on your radar.

However, you can:

1. Use paving stones for your patio to allow the water to seep down into the soil and not run off into the streets or alleys.
2. If you do have a garden, rotate your plants each season to keep the nutrients from becoming depleted.
3. Help your community by planting trees because the tree roots penetrate deeply into the soil which helps to bring mineral up into the soil.
4. Not pour chemical solutions onto your grass; take them to your local hazardous waste recycling station.

All That WATER and There Is a Problem

As 70 percent of the planet is covered by water one would think clean drinking water would not be a societal issue. However, 97 percent of that water is contained within the oceans leaving only about 3 percent of this water as fresh water. The majority (69 percent) of the fresh water is ice, frozen in the glaciers and polar ice caps.[15]

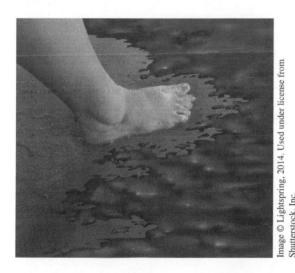

Image © Lightspring, 2014. Used under license from Shutterstock, Inc.

Image © Tracing Tea, 2014. Used under license from Shutterstock, Inc.

Much like the contamination of our soils, as the population grew in villages there was a greater need for fresh water for drinking, cooking, and cleaning—thus more people moved along streams and rivers for easier access. Bathing, cleaning of dishes and clothes, and drinking often came from the same sources of water.

In several tribes and villages around the world to this day, human defecation of young children in an open area, on the ground, or in a body of water is still common practice until they become "potty-trained"—however, in some cases as they get older the "potty" is often a hole in a dock (surrounded by a tarp as a make-shift privy) over a body of water. The same body of water in which children and adults can be seen bathing and swimming a few hundred feet away.[16]

In addition to human contamination, agricultural pesticides and industrial waste has seeped into the freshwater supply making the water hazardous to health. Globally we use 70 percent of our water sources for agriculture and 19 percent for industry leaving very little for drinking water and other personal needs.[17]

The most prevalent chemical contaminant in the world's groundwater is nitrate because of the widespread use of commercial fertilizers and human waste. Nitrates in drinking water is often related to urine nitrate levels. Water with high nitrate concentration is not suitable for human consumption and is possibly carcinogenic in humans. High level of nitrates is one of the major concerns in the water supply in Iran.[18]

The World Health Organization (2010) reports that there are almost one billion people who do not have access to clean safe water with 37 percent of those people living in Sub-Saharan Africa. In addition, approximately 7 million Iraqis have little or no safe water to drink, which ranks Iraq the 5th worst country in the world for safe water. As of August 17, 2011, globally one out of five children under the age of 5 dies due to water-related diseases.[19] While the 2000 Millennium Development Goal Target 7c seeks to reduce by half the proportion of the population without sustainable access to safe drinking water, current projections believe we will fall short and over a billion people will not have safe drinking water.[20] The major reason for this shortfall will be the continued open defecation practices in many countries. An acceptable practice without much notice to the health consequences for humanity.

Another culprit polluting our waters over the past few decades is the addition of pharmaceuticals including antibiotics, heart medications, and psychotropic. Often, these outdated and no-longer-needed products are tossed into our toilets without thought to where they go[21]—in addition, pharmaceuticals also enter wastewater systems because medications are only partially absorbed by the body and the residues are excreted. While almost one billion people go without clean water, which leads to communicable diseases, many of us simply go to the faucet or open the refrigerator and grab a bottle of clean drinking water without thinking how precious this resource has become. Many of us take for granted what may one day be the next gold—fresh drinking water.

Below is a list of practical solutions for how you can protect our water.

The water conservation hierarchy established by most governments is pretty simply: reduce, reuse, and recycle.

You can:

1. Take shorter showers.
2. Use water-efficient appliances like front-loading washing machines, dual-flush toilets, and low-flow showerheads.
3. Plant water-efficient plants.
4. Reuse rainwater and greywater.
5. Do not flush pharmaceuticals.
6. Dispose of chemical cleaners, solvents, and oil. responsibly – not down your drains.
7. Use car washes that recycle the wash water.

What Are We Breathing in Our Air?

Breathing is one of the most important human functions on earth—however, like soil and water contamination, air pollution has increased with population growth and the growth of agriculture and industrialization creating lung conditions and difficulty in breathing for many people. Exposure to airborne particulate matter has been associated with increase in mortality and hospital admissions due to respiratory and cardiovascular disease.[22]

The quality of the air is determined by the amount of indoor air pollution and outdoor urban air pollution.

Image © Minerva Studio, 2014. Used under license from Shutterstock, Inc.

The leading causes of outdoor urban air pollution are chemical and coal-fired plants, oil refineries, incinerators, large livestock farms, and motor vehicle emissions.[23]

Billions of people inhale smoke, fossil-fuel emissions, and car exhaust in the form of outdoor urban air pollution on a daily basis. Traffic congestion is a major environmental stressor that increases vehicle emissions and degrades air quality around the world. Although our understanding of the impact of air pollution is very limited, recent studies have shown excess mortality and morbidity rates in not only drivers but individuals living and working near major highways as well.[24]

In major cities vehicle emissions adds carbon monoxide (CO), carbon dioxide (CO_2), hydrocarbons (HCs), nitrogen oxides (NOx), and particulate matter (PM) to our air.[24] The marginal risks from exposure to these toxins are exacerbated by the amount of congestion, road types, and exposure locations. These determinants make it difficult for air quality management and policy making related to traffic because there is no consistency in the risks to human health.

Despite these difficulties in air quality management, a recent report stated that of the 3.2 million premature deaths are attributed to air pollution worldwide, 1.2 million of them occurred in China.[24] In China, the fourth leading cause of death is from PM just behind dietary risks, high blood pressure, and smoking.

Many of those affected are children because much of their lives are spent outdoors. Their active lives are spent running and playing which brings the polluted air deep into their little undeveloped lungs. This study also found significantly lower developmental scores and reduced motor development in 2-year-olds who were exposed to coal-burning emissions during their gestation period.

Besides the outdoor air pollution, almost half of the world's population still relies on solid fuels, biomass, and coal for their everyday energy needs such as cooking, heat, and light for the houses.[26] In the early settlements of the United States, "buffalo wood" and "cow wood" could be seen piled up against the houses much like tree wood is today. Fortunately, dung is not used in many homes in America today.

Nonetheless, inefficient cooking stoves used in many yurts, tent, and houses around the world fill homes with dense black smoke that puts inhabitants at risk of pneumonia, lung cancer, and chronic obstructive pulmonary disease. Since most of the cooking is done by women, surrounded by their children, they are at greatest risk for the adverse health effects from these fires.[26]

One of the major sources of fuel is dung which is dried excrement from large wild and domesticated animals, such as buffalo, cows, and yaks. Dung is used in most of the Middle East, Egypt, Africa, and the high-altitude regions of North and South America.[27]

Presently in the high plateau areas of Tibet, one of the most remote areas of the world, millions of Tibetans follow the traditional nomadic lifestyle living in yak wool tents and burning yak dung for heat and cooking.

Image © Tracing Tea, 2014. Used under license from Shutterstock, Inc.

Almost three-fourths of the total energy in the northern Tibet Plateau (natural pasture) are from yak dung, wood, and strew whereas in the southern plateau (forests and farmland) they mostly use wood and strew.[28]

The smoke from these biomass sources generates much more smoke than burning seasoned wood and is a major cause of indoor air pollution in some parts of the world. Despite efforts such as the United Nations Foundation Global Alliance for Clean Cookstoves, a public–private partnership aimed at creating a global market for efficient cooking stoves, indoor air pollutants from primitive cooking stoves used in the developing world contribute to nearly 2 million deaths a year.[29] More research is needed to determine the amount of reduction in indoor air pollution that is required to improve health and to evaluate the benefits of programs already under way.

We can conclude that both outdoor and indoor air pollutants are associated with health issues such as respiratory and cardiovascular disease, lung cancer, aggravated bronchitis, asthma, and premature death. Many of these health issues tend to increase the amount of daily stress an individual experiences which often decreases their overall well-being.

Below is a list of practical solutions for how you can protect our air.

1. Carpool and drive your car less.
2. Use public transportation – buses and light rail.
3. Encourage your public transportation companies to update the vehicles with cleaner fuel vehicles.
4. Bike to work or school.
5. If you must drive your car, ensure that the engine is always tuned up.
6. Choose fuel-efficient vehicles.
7. Follow your local "no-burn" day advisories when they are communicated.

Impact of Global Environmental Stress

Image © Leah-Anne Thompson, 2014. Used under license from Shutterstock, Inc.

Human health is strongly connected to the environment of our planet—thus, contaminated soil, water, and air have a tremendous impact on, not only the health of our planet, but the health and well-being of humanity as well. When the earth is stressed it relieves its stress by delivering massive earth changes such as volcanoes and earthquakes caused by tectonic shifts in the earth's plates, as well as changes in weather patterns. When a human is stressed the result is most often physical and emotional disease—in fact, it has been suggested that environmental stressors such as soil, water, and air pollution may represent the greatest public health challenge the humanity has ever faced. Discovery of the environmental exposure is of paramount importance to our planet as these pollutants influence human health before conception and all throughout one's life.[30]

Thus considering the rapid urbanization of countries and increasing levels of pollution, clean soil, water, and air needs to be a global priority for the continuation of a healthy productive planet. Public health and regulatory policies for environmental protection should be a component of the educational curriculum of health care professionals as well as integrated into the priorities of any primary health care system.

An example of environmental policy in the United States is The Clean Air Act which is the law that requires the US Environmental Protection Agency (EPA) to set national air-quality standards for PM and five other pollutants considered harmful to the public health and the environment[31]—this framework for air quality protects Americans from harmful air pollutants and attempts to mitigate respiratory and cardiac disease that has increased hospital admissions over the years.

In addition to the world governments creating policies and laws to curb the global pollution, organizations have been created to address these daunting issues. Years ago an American theorist, inventor, and futurist, Buckminster Fuller during his 1972–1973 lecture tour at the University of California was heard many times stating, "You never change things by fighting the existing reality. To change something, build a NEW model that makes the existing model obsolete."[32] We are now in the process of building new models for cleaning up the soil, water, and air pollution around the world.

One of the largest organizations and websites, with over 20 million viewers, representing a new model is called the Solution Hub. Foster Gamble and his wife, Kimberly have created a new model for creating change in the world. They are attempting to answer the question, what in the world would it take for us to thrive instead of simply surviving?

Experts from around the world have gathered to share information in the Solution Hub made up of twelve sectors including arts, science, health science, spirituality, etc. One frequently visited sector is the environment where the vision is of "a healthy planet, free of pollution where people act responsibly to protect and maintain balance with the environment"[33]

A list, beyond the scope of this chapter, of websites and magazines are filled with different ideas and do-it-yourself (DIY) projects on how you can make a difference in the world. Whole issues are written to discuss how we can grow and eat healthy food through organic gardening, how to have clean water, discussions on renewable energies, and how we can cut our carbon footprints by taking tiny steps. Two of the author's favorites are like Yes! Magazine[34] and Mother Earth News[35] that are always filled with current global success stories and ideas. Projects also exist for almost any issue you might be interested in addressing regarding soil, water, and air pollution around the world. Are you concerned about safe drinking water in sub-Saharan Africa[36] or what about the drinking water in Iraq?[37] Do you want to know if the soil is contaminated, how do we create new soil?[38] Becoming a part of a global solution is as simple as starting a search online and then registering to participate.

We all agree that changes need to be made—and the above examples listed are good ways to start but we need to emphasize that any change in a community, nation, or world starts with the individual becoming responsible and productive citizens. If we review Maslow's hierarchy of needs, an individual cannot live in a stressful environment and be responsible and productive citizens. Changing the amount of environmental stress on a global level could take the personal stressors out of one's life possibly leading to self-reliance and personal responsibility. Self-reliant individuals could become the solution rather than the problem.

Image © alphaspirit, 2014. Used under license from Shutterstock, Inc.

The Solution: Be the Solution

As one humanity, we face global challenges. Our old ways of doing things have brought us to the edge of a grand precipice . . . and we are about to fall off. We have forgotten how to take care of our planet, our home, and each other. To paraphrase Albert Einstein, no problem can be solved from the same level of consciousness that created it.[39] The bright light is that collective consciousness is awakening with new desires involving a transformation of how we do things around the world.

The solutions to the Impact of Global Environmental Stress on Universal Well-Being are only as limited as our collective creative minds. This author contends that, becoming part of the solution comes in three stages. First, the individual must simply become aware of what is going on around the world with regard to environmental issues. Reading this chapter is a great beginning in awareness, and watching the YouTube video on Ten Worst Pollution Problems in the World can provide you with further information.[40]

The second stage requires a greater consciousness in order to wake up to the environmental injustices in this world. Dominelli (2012) defined environmental justice as being surrounded by a myriad of

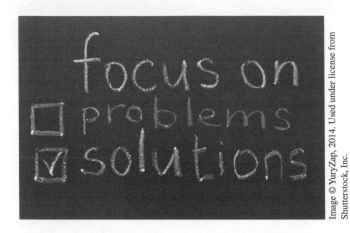

Image © YuryZap, 2014. Used under license from Shutterstock, Inc.

controversial issues. She revealed how lower social economic status leads to more exposure to the effects of environmental pollution. These are the same poor communities which become dumping grounds for toxic industrial waste and have their forests, jungles, and rainforests stripped of precious resources in the name of progress.[41]

An open mind is needed to enter the second stage of waking up to what is going on in our world today. By developing an understanding of how consumerism and greed has led to many of the global environmental issues, one's perceptions of the issues often change. Often a greater understanding is gleaned by visiting third world countries and mingling with its inhabitants. Inhabitants that have the same desire for productive soil, fresh water, clean air, and happiness that we all do.

By questioning one's beliefs and perceptions a mind begins to expand to see the world in new ways—from this new worldview is where all the solutions arise to these global environmental stressors.

Image © Jag_cz, 2014. Used under license from Shutterstock, Inc.

The last stage is the most difficult and few people around the world have ventured into this unknown arena. In the final stage, one needs to let go of all their current beliefs, perceptions, judgments, and ego—leave their past behind them and focus with laser-like intention on creating a new world for the greater good of all men and women.

In order to create this new world several methods can be utilized with a disciplined mind. Becoming the solution becomes a real possibility once we understand the power within ourselves to create our own reality. That power comes from our thoughts. The author's first exposure to thoughts being things was over thirty years ago when creating "Breakfasts with Champions" workshops with pioneers in positive mental attitudes and thought processing such as Norman Vincent Peale, Don Hutchinson, Charlie Tremendous Jones, Mark Victor Hanson, and other pioneers. This was the beginning to a lifelong search for a greater meaning to life.

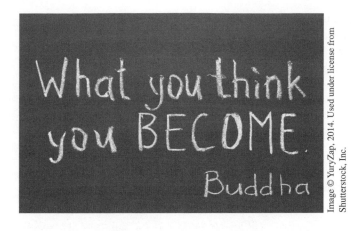

Image © YuryZap, 2014. Used under license from Shutterstock, Inc.

Once we learn that every thought we have has its consequence in our life[42] we open our minds to a whole new reality. Every thought we have produces a biochemical reaction in our brain. Then our brain releases chemicals into our body which are messengers that are matched with feelings. As a result, when we think happy thoughts our brain manufactures chemicals that make us feel joyful.[43]

Meditation and Visualization are two of the most powerful ways to open our minds to a new reality—with meditation, participants enter into a state of being where a higher level of consciousness can be received—this is the state where most inventors, authors, and designers go—aha, I have got it! This is the state where many believe the magic of the Universe begins.

When you meditate, adding a visualization of the future you want to see sends the creative power back to the Universe. Focusing on what you want and not on what you do not want has a profound effect on one's life. In her daily practice, the author sees a world filled with love and joy in which all people live in radiant health with clean water and fresh air; free energy; and abundance for all.

By meditating and visualizing on a daily basis, individuals often find they wake up in a state of joy and experience the blissful living discussed by Napoli in the prologue of this book. We will end this chapter with one last powerful thought by amending the late United States president John F. Kennedy's famous words to—ask not what your world can do for you, but what you can do for your world.[44]

"Anything else you're interested in is not going to happen if you can't breathe the air and drink the water. Don't sit this one out. Do something. You are by accident of fate alive at an absolutely critical moment in the history of our planet."[45]

References

1. Maslow Abraham, *Towards the Psychology of Being,* 2d ed. NY: Van Nostrand, 1968.

2. www.Merriam-Webster.com.

3. World Economic Forum, *Well-being and Global Success,* 2012, 4. http://www3.weforum.org/docs/WEF_HE_GAC_WellbeingGlobalSuccess_Report 2012.pdf.

4. Hippocrates, *Hippocratic Writings* (Edited with an introduction by G.E.R. Lloyd). Harmondsworth: Penguin, 1978.

5. Rath, T. & Harter, J., *Well-Being: The Five Essential Elements.* New York, NY: Gallup Press, 2010.

6. Cornell University, Pollution Causes 40 Percent of Death Worldwide. *Science Daily,* 2007. www.sciencedaily.com/releases/2007/08/070813162438.htm.

7. Hartmann, T., *The Last Hours of Ancient Sunlight.* New York: Three Rivers Press, 2004.

8. www.worldometers.info/world-population.

9. Kellogg, Charles F., "Soil," *Scientific American* 183 (1950): 30–39.

10. http://historylink101.com/lessons/farm-city/story-of-farming.htm.

11. Dirt Poor: Have Fruits and Vegetables Become Less Nutritious? Scientific American, 2004. http://www.scientificamerican.com/article.cfm?id=soild-depletion-and-nutrition-loss.

12. Henao, J. & Baanante, C., *Estimating Rates of Nutrient Depletion in Soils of Agricultural Lands of Africa.* Muscle Shoals, AL: *Technical Bulletin* IFDC-T-48, 1999. http://pdf.usaid.gov/pdf_docs/PNADW837.pdf.

13. Mendona, M. L., "Monocropping for Agrofuels: The Case of Brazil," *Development* 54 no. (1) (2011): 98–103. doi:http://dx.doi.org/10.1057/dev.2010.100.

14. European Environment Agency, Progress in Management of Contaminated Sites (CSI 015)—Assessment Published, 2007. http://www.eea.europa.eu/data-and-maps/indicators/progress-in-management-of-contaminated-sites/progress-in-management-of-contaminated.

15. http://www.universetoday.com/65588/what-percent-of-earth-is-water/#ixzz2hpgSF1bT.

16. Personal experiences in Peru and along the Amazon in 2006 and later in Africa, south of Botswana in 2009.

17. AQUASTAT, Food and Agriculture Organization of the United Nations. Water Use, 2012. http://www.fao.org/nr/water/aquastat/water_use/index.stm.

18. Samaneh Khademikia, Zahra Rafiee, Mohammad Mehdi Amin, Parinaz Poursafa, Marjan Mansourian, & Amir Modaberi, Association of nitrate, nitrite, and total organic carbon (TOC) in drinking water and gastrointestinal disease," *Journal of Environmental and Public Health* (2013): 1–4. Article ID 603468. doi:10.1155/2013/603468.

19. WHO/UNICEF (Joint Monitoring Programme for Water Supply and Sanitation). "Progress on Sanitation and Drinking Water," 2010. www.wssinfo.org/.

20. Basingstoke, *Achieving the Millennium Development Goals.* Edited by Mark McGillivray, 2008. Palgrave Macmillan in association with the United Nations University—World Institute for Development Economics Research.

21. Leitman, M., "Water R[x]: The Problem of Pharmaceuticals in Our Nation's Waters," *UCLA Journal of Environmental Law and Policy* 29 (2011): 395.

22. Brunekreef, B. & Holgate, S. T., "Air Pollution and Health," *Lancet* 360 9341 (2002): 1233–1242. http://www.sciencedirect.com.ezproxy1.lib.asu.edu/science/article/pii/S0140673602112748.

23. Environmental Performance Report 2001. https://www.unilever.com/Images/2001-unilever-environmental-performance-summary-report_tcm244-409700_1_en.pdf

24. Zhang, K. & Batterman, S., "Air Pollution and Health Risks Due to Vehicle Traffic," *Science of the Total Environment* 450–451 (2013): 307–16. http://www.sciencedirect.com/science/article/pii/S0048969713001290.

25. Finamore, B., Air Pollution in China: The Kids aren't Alright. *The Energy Collective*, April 6, 2013. http://theenergycollective.com/barbarafinamore/206431/kids-arent-alright-China-air-pollution.

26. World Health Organization (WHO), Indoor Air Pollution and Health. Fact Sheet #292, 2011. http://www.who.int/mediacentre/factsheets/fs292/en/.

27. DUNG, In Berkshire encyclopedia of sustainability: Natural resources and sustainability, 2001. https://literate.credoreference.com.exproxy1.lib.asu.edu./content/entry/berkshrs/dung/0.

28. Kang, S., Li, C., Wany, F., Zhang, Q., & Cong, Z., "Total Suspended Particulate Matter and Toxic Elements Indoors During Cooking with Yak Dung," *Atmospheric Environment* 43 no. (27) (2009): 42243–46. http://dx.doi.org/10.1016/j.atmosenv.2009.06.015.

29. Friedrich M. J., "Reducing Indoor Air Pollution," *Journal of American Medical Association* 306 no. (23) (2011): 2553. doi:10.1001/jama.2011.1807.

30. Roya K., Amin, M. M., Haghdoost, A. A., Gupta, A. K. & Tuhkanen, T. A., "Pollutants Source Control and Health Effects," *Journal of Environmental and Public Health* (2013). Article ID 209739. doi:10.1155/2013/209739.

31. Huan, B., "The Clean Air Act," *Chest* 140 no. (1) (2011):1–2. doi:10.1378/chest.11-1018.

32. http://www.goodreads.com/author/quotes/165737.Richard_Buckminster_Fuller.

33. www.thrivemovement.com.

34. www.yesmagazine.org.

35. *www.motherearthnews.com.*

36. www.thewaterproject.org.

37. www.reconciliationproject.org.

38. http://www.motherearthnews.com/organic-gardening/gardening-techniques/complete-organic-fertilizer-zebz1309znsp.aspx

39. http://rescomp.stanford.edu/~cheshire/EinsteinQuotes.html.

40. http://www.mnn.com/earth-matters/wilderness-resources/photos/the-10-worst-pollution-problems-in-the-world/bad-form.

41. Dominelli, L., *Green Social Work: From Environmental Crises to Environmental Justice.* Cambridge, UK: Polarity Press, 2012.

42. Holmes, E. & Kinnear, W., *Thoughts are Things.* Deerfield Beach, FL: Health Communications Inc, 1967.

43. Dispenza, J., *Evolve Your Brain: The Science of Changing Your Mind.* Deerfield Beach, FL: Health Communications Inc., 2007, 42–46.

44. http://www.goodreads.com/author/quotes/3047.John_F_Kennedy.

45. (www.wisdomquotes.com/quote/carl-sagan-8.html)

KNOWLEDGE LEARNED

Activities

1. Turn on an outside faucet and fill a glass of water. Examine the water: look at it, smell it, taste it. Now contemplate the idea that almost 1:7 people in the world do not have clean, safe drinking water. What does that mean to you?

2. Light a fire in a safe place—add some wet wood (or better yet, cow dung) to the fire to make it smoky. How are you breathing? Contemplate having this fire inside your home and cooking your evening meal on it like half the people in the world.

3. Find a recipe for "dirt" and make a container full. Now plant a tomato, pepper, or some herbs in the container. See if the food tastes different than what you buy from the grocery store.

4. Go to www.thrivemovement.com and peruse the 12 sectors identified. What is the vision of the environmental sector?

5. Read one article listed under the topic "pollution" in the environmental sector of the Thrive Movement. Did reading this article change something inside of you?

6. Watch The Story of Stuff http://www.youtube.com/watch?v=9GorqroigqM. How does this story of stuff relate to this chapter?

7. List three things that you will make a commitment to change with regard to global environmental stress.

8. Go to www.kindspring.org/ideas/ under the heading Environment there are 20 ideas—pick one.

9. Practice visualizing by getting into a meditative state and then imagining a recent meal or happy moment. Bring in as many senses as you can, like smells of the food, feelings of grass on your feet, etc.

Questions

1. Does well-being increase the productivity of workers and profitability of the companies in which they work? If so, how?

2. Is there a correlation between environmental pollution and the growth in world population? Explain.

3. What percentage of deaths worldwide are caused by water, air, and soil pollution do to environmental degradation?

4. According to Thom Harmann, how many years did it take to reach our first billion people in this world?

5. Before farming, how did people eat?

6. What percentage of our earth is covered by water?

7. How much of our fresh water is used for agriculture and irrigation?

8. What effect did crop yield have on the depletion of nutrients in soil?

9. Name two chemicals that are found in soils that should not be there.

10. What is your thinking about thoughts?

11. If the global environmental stress issues were resolved, what effect would it have on Universal well-being?

MINDFUL AWARENESS REFLECTION JOURNAL

Choose one mindful experience as you begin your reflection.

Empathically Acknowledge

Describe your experience

_____

_____

_____

Intentional Attention

Describe what you noticed

Breath
Body
Emotions
Thoughts
Senses

Accept Without Judgment

Describe judgment; acceptance

_____

_____

_____

Willingly Choose

Intention/willingness; new perspective

_____

_____

_____

Mindful Mac Meditation

Describe your meditation experiences. What did you learn?

_____

_____

_____

CHAPTER CRITICAL THINKING AND ACTIVITY JOURNAL

This is an opportunity for you to fully describe your thoughts, opinions and experience following the reading and activities.

The most important information/key concepts we need to understand from these chapters are:

_____

_____

_____

_____

How can I use the information in the chapters to help me with my daily mindfulness practice?

_____

_____

_____

_____

In what ways will the material learned in these chapters help me manage my stress more effectively?

_____

_____

_____

_____

What are your thoughts and feedback regarding the information and activities for each chapter?

_____

_____

_____

_____

CHAPTER SIX

THE SCIENCE OF INSTINCTS AND INTUITION
Intuitive Smartness in Times of Information Overload
By Jonas Nordstrom

Courtesy of Ryan Dow

Picture is reproduced with permission.[1]

My monkey mind is quiet
There is room in my brain
I am paying attention
I am clear

Maria Napoli

Long before we began using the Internet with all its various sources of information, such as social medias, blogs, Wikipedia, Google, and YouTube, well-renowned futurist Alvin Toffler[2] wrote as early as in 1970 in his bestselling book *Future Shock* that,

In the three short decades between now and the twenty-first century, millions of ordinary, psychologically normal people will face an abrupt collision with the future. Citizens of the world's richest and most technologically advanced nations, many of them will find it increasingly painful to keep up with the incessant demand for change that characterizes our time. For them, the future will have arrived too soon.[2(p.9)]

Image © Elnur, 2014. Used under license from Shutterstock, Inc.

In the accelerated process of undergoing structural changes from an *industrial society* to an *information society*, people are being overwhelmed by information. To function effectively during such circumstances, an individual depends upon the power to predict, at least to a fair degree, the outcome of one's actions.[2] However, when exposed to information overload, an individual's predictive accuracy decreases radically—as compensation, it is necessary to either *process for more information* than before, or *develop new strategies* for making efficient decisions. As you begin this chapter take a moment to reflect upon your experience of being stressed out and overwhelmed by information.

An indication that we have not yet succeeded in adapting to processing information faster and at larger quantities is revealed in a historical comparison of stress levels across the USA. From 1983 to 2009 stress increased 18 percent for women and 24 percent for men,[3] supporting Toffler's ideas about a *Future Shocked* society. These findings also reveal that the younger an individual is, the higher the levels of stress they are experiencing.[3] The main reasons for why stress levels are much higher today than 25 years ago are that," Economic pressures are greater, and it's harder to turn off information, and it's harder to buffer ourselves from the world."[4]

Thus, in order to avoid becoming stressed out, turning off information, and buffering ourselves from the world, current and coming generations need to develop new approaches for choosing and managing information. Since information overload occurs when the cognitive processing capacity is exceeded by the amount of input,[5] it would be appealing if one could reduce the amount of input and still make sound decisions. This is actually something that has been found in occupations where one needs to make decisions on short notice with limited amount of information, such as entrepreneurs, pilots, firemen, and military personnel. The key aspect has been to *include the use of intuition* in the operational work.

As an example, in the United States Army Field Manual on Command and Control (FM 101-5) a section on *intuitive decision making* is included.[6] It has been shown that by including the intuition in the military planning guide, planning time can be significantly reduced without sacrificing quality.[7] A similar model for *intuitive decision making* has become standard for tactical decision making in the Swedish Armed Forces.[8]

Understanding Intuitive Smartness

In this chapter, a model for *intuitive decision making* will be presented that intends to assist the reader in learning to choose and make decisions in times of information overload. This model is called *Intuitive Smartness (IS)*. IS primarily expands from two different frameworks; the naturalistic decision making

(NDM) model and the mind-boggling research relating to noetic science and nonlocal intuition. While the NDM framework focuses primarily "on the way people build expertise and apply it to cognitive functions such as judgment and decision making,"[9] noetic science uses rigorous scientific methods "to study the nature of direct inner knowing and the boundaries between the subjective and the objective."[10]

By combining the NDM model with the research relating to noetic science, IS is designed to use the idea that intuitive perception is based on an individual's unconscious mind accessing information from *prior experiences and the ability to recognize various patterns*, as in NDM, as well as the human possibility to intuitively perceive information from a distant or future source, as has been demonstrated in the field of noetic science.[11–13] Thus, IS intends to teach the practitioner how to use the intuition to *access one's direct inner knowing*, which is the actual meaning of the Greek word *noetikus*.[10]

However, before deepening our knowledge about the intuition, we will examine how intuition is related to animal and human instincts. Like all animals in the animal kingdom, we as mammals possess instincts. Yet as humans, most people no longer have fine-tuned instincts due to a large dependence on receiving information from language and machines. Therefore, let us take a moment to understand a bit more about instincts and how we can recapture our inherent ability to instinctually respond to our experiences.

Instincts and the Inheritance from the Animal Kingdom

Image © Vishnevskiy Vasily, 2014. Used under license from Shutterstock, Inc.

In the field of behavioral science, the instinct is "generally understood as the innate part of behavior that emerges without any training or education in humans"[14]—that means that an instinct is a *natural ability* that makes an organism act in a particular way *without needing to learn it or think about it*.[15]

One fundamental instinct is the self-preservation instinct and the sexual instinct—while the self-preservation instinct helps us to either avoid or respond to danger, such as in the fight, flight, or freeze response, the sexual instinct plays a vital function in animal and human reproduction. Instinctual reactions are typically automatic, due to being governed by the older parts of the brain, located in the brainstem and the limbic system. Responding intuitively, on the other hand, involves processing instinctual data using logical and analytical reasoning, associated with newer parts of the brain, such as the neocortex.

Animals Detecting Danger through Their Instincts

To better understand the purpose of human instincts, let us investigate the role instincts have for animals in detecting danger. British biologist Rupert Sheldrake has written extensively about how animals are able to anticipate disasters and sense impending danger with the help of their instincts.[16] For example, he discovered that animals were behaving as if they were able to sense when an earthquake was about to happen. Sheldrake describes,

"Some cats were said to be hiding for no apparent reason up to 12 hours before the earthquake; others were behaving in an anxious way or 'freaking out' an hour or two before; some dogs were barking "frantically" before the earthquake struck; and goats and other animals were showing obvious signs of fear."[16(p.1)]

Sheldrake, as well as Chinese researchers, have found that numerous animals also behave in a similar way before avalanches, tsunamis, as well as man-made disasters such as military air raids. As an example, in relation to the tsunami occurring in the Indian Ocean on December 26, 2004, elephants, leopards, monkeys, and birds miraculously were reported to escape by seeking refuge in higher terrain[17]—thus, instincts seem to play a vital role for animals to detect danger, even ahead of time, and as a result be able to successfully escape into safety. Humans may not be tuned to their instincts on such a deep level, yet our bodies are continually communicating with us, offering information to help us make accurate decisions, and yes, even prevent danger or unpleasant experiences.

Subconsciously Reacting to Danger Ahead of Time

Similarly to animals, the human autonomic nervous system responds to danger even before it happens. While nothing specific happens when watching a calm picture, the autonomic nervous system reacts several seconds *before* seeing a threatening picture. For instance, the electrodermal activity of the heart changes approximately four to seven seconds ahead of seeing a threatening picture.[11,18–22] Imagine that!

When a functional magnetic resonance imaging (fMRI) was used to reveal which part of the brain was active before and during seeing the threatening picture, the result revealed that regions near the amygdala, which is a part of the limbic system, were particularly active.[23] Since these regions are involved in processing threat and sensory data with an emotional content, such as fear and rage, one may conclude that the emotional picture activated a stress response in the test subject.

Image © imagineerinx, 2014. Used under license from Shutterstock, Inc.

When measuring the electric activity of the brain and the heart, with the help of electroencephalography (EEG) respectively electrocardiography (ECG), the results revealed "that the heart appears to receive intuitive information [about 1.3 seconds] before the brain,"[20] something that will be important to remember further on when practicing how to use intuition. These findings suggest that instinctual foreknowledge involves perception of implicit information by the body's psychophysiological systems, something that will be examined more in depth further ahead. However, before that, a quick question: Did you ever feel that someone was staring at you without actually seeing the person? Maybe you thought you were losing your mind, yet, research has shown that maybe your were right on!

Instinctively Detecting When Being Stared at

Another aspect of detecting danger is that both animals and humans seem to be able to instinctively detect when they are being stared at. For instance, unconscious effects have been measured in the autonomic nervous system when an individual is being stared at.[24,25] Interestingly enough, it seems like the autonomic nervous system is reacting even when the person watching is looking through a closed-circuit television (CCTV).

Sheldrake argues that the ability to detect when being stared at is part of a natural survival mechanism, originally alerting prey animals when a predator is looking at them.[26–28] When Sheldrake investigated if it was possible to *consciously* sense when being stared at, in addition to the *unconscious* effects reported above, he found that the individual being stared at was able to guess right in 54.7 percent of the time, compared to 50 percent expected by chance.

When the test subjects were given a chance to receive feedback, whether they were guessing right or wrong, the scores drastically improved—for instance, eight to nine year old children in a German school, after having received training, were able to achieve an accuracy of as high as 90 percent. Since these results reveal that it is possible to learn how to become aware of unconscious instinctual information, they also indicate that *intuition is a skill* that can be enhanced through training.[29] What a treat to have this amazing tool to help us navigate through life's experiences!

Image © fufu10, 2014. Used under license from Shutterstock, Inc.

To conclude this section, we have learned that instincts, and foremost the self-preservation instinct, play a vital role in detecting implicit information relating to danger. When the autonomic nervous system is receiving and processing large amounts of sensory impressions, it appears that the human organism is even able to perceive beyond the traditional boundaries of space and time. The next topic to investigate is how instinctual responses are part of the intuitive decision making process, as well as to find out how the self-preservation instinct and the sexual instinct also can compromise and distort true intuitive impressions.

Intuition and the Intuitive Genius Within

One major difference between instinct and intuition is that instinct is associated with automatic responses *below the conscious level*, while intuition is a refined process in which unconscious data has been processed and presented as *conscious hunches, insights, or understandings*. This means that the intuition is "a process that gives us the ability to know something directly without analytic reasoning, bridging the gap between the conscious and unconscious parts of our mind, and also between instinct and reason."[30] By learning to acknowledge information related to our instincts, gut feelings, and hunches, and subsequently combining these valuable impressions with analytical reasoning, an individual can learn to make intuitive decisions and become very adaptive in a world of rapid changes.

Researchers have studied individuals that need to make critical decisions under difficult conditions, such as intensive care personnel, military pilots, and firemen.[9,31] Klein and his team found that when conditions were unstable, time was limited, and the stakes were high, some individuals were still able to perform exceptionally well. To the researchers' big surprise, they discovered that instead of using analogical reasoning and comparing different options, the key point was to use instinct and intuition.

Expert Intuition in Firemen

When studying firemen commanders in their natural environment, it became evident to Klein that some of the commanders just intuitively knew what to do—the key aspect was to *recognize familiar patterns* in what was happening around them. Instead of asking, "What do I do now?" the commanders asked themselves, "What is going on here?" The commanders then used their experience to assess the situation, match relevant cues to patterns they had already learned, and then decide the best course of action. This is something you too can do! It can be easy when you are mindful, quiet the "monkey mind" and pay attention to your "gut."

Although the researchers initially were biased to find that the commanders were wrestling with different choices and struggling with comparing them to each other, as described in various formal decision making processes, the results clearly demonstrated that they did not need to do that—instead, after having used their imagination to internally experience if an option would work or not, the commanders went along with *the first identified* reasonable action—that means that the commanders could immediately rule out an action if it did not intuitively feel right to them, or go ahead if it seemed to be the right one, and as a result save a lot of valuable time.

This process is referred to as *mental simulation,* and is defined as, "the ability to imagine people and objects consciously and to transform those people and objects through several transitions, finally picturing them in a different way than at the start."[31(p.45)] Mental simulation was studied in chess masters as early as 1946 and has been found to be a crucial strategy for making successful decisions. Just as

Image © marekuliasz, 2014. Used under license from Shutterstock, Inc.

chess masters use their imagination to play out a sequence of actions and then determine if that sequence is doable or not, successful business leaders, entrepreneurs, airline pilots, anesthesiologists, nurses, and military officers do the same.[9,32,33]

By using prior knowledge and experience to rapidly recognize familiar patterns and scenarios, these experts did not need to make their mental simulations very elaborate—instead, the experts seemed to play out the scenario through only a few different transition states. Often it was sufficient to use only two or three key factors in each transition state, making it possible to run through the scenario without getting stuck in unnecessary details and as a consequence lose valuable time.

"Felt Sense" and How Intuitive Impressions Are Experienced

To better understand this automatic and subconscious process of recognizing patterns, we can compare it to spelling or reading a word. When reading an incorrect spelled word, most people often automatically sense that something is wrong. For instance, when you read the words "shcool," "uƨe," and "mispelled," the brain often automatically recognizes the incorrect spelling and a subtle sensation is created, informing us that something is wrong. On the other hand, when the words are spelled correctly, as in "school," "use," and "misspelled," the brain automatically compares the word to the earlier learned correct spelling, and a subtle, often not even noticeable, positive or familiar sensation is created.

The perception of these subtle sensations is referred to as "felt sense." The term refers to the discovery psychotherapist Eugene Gendlin did when he discovered that successful patients of psychotherapy intuitively focus on subtle internal bodily impressions, containing information about how to resolve the problem the client is experiencing.[34] These impressions are preconceptual, meaning they exist before any mental constructions, abstractions, or generalizations are created about a particular, lived experience.

By using felt sense, intuitive impressions can be experienced on four different levels: the physical, emotional, mental, and universal level.[35]

The first level of intuitive signals relates to the *physical level* of awareness and includes physical sensations, such as *gut feelings, tensions, tingling sensations, or various kinds of pain*; for example, in the stomach or in the head. The second level of intuitive signals is the *emotional level*, conveying intuitive information in the form of sudden *changes of feelings*, or an immediate *attraction* or *aversion* for something without logically understanding why. The third level of intuitive signals relates to the *mental level* of awareness and includes mental *insights*, immediate *comprehensions*, or sudden *flashes of knowledge*. On the fourth level, *the universal level*, also referred to as the spiritual level, the impressions often come as a *greater understanding*, with a sense of a *grander interconnectedness* between different ideas, issues, or individuals. Now use *exercise one* to better understand the experience of felt sense.

Exercise 1—Felt Sense

1. Think about a person you dislike, or irritated at, or hold any other negative feelings towards.
   a. How does your body react (tension, posture, breathing)?
   b. How do you feel emotionally?
   c. What thoughts come to your mind?

2. Think about a person you like, or thankful to, or hold any other positive feelings towards.
   a. How does your body react (contract/relax, warm/cold)?
   b. How do you feel emotionally?
   c. What thoughts come to your mind?

3. How does your felt sense differ in the above examples?

4. What level (physical, emotional, or mental) was easiest to perceive for you?

Image © ollyy, 2014. Used under license from Shutterstock, Inc.

Receiving Nonlocal Information

Although most intuitive information probably is related to an individual's expertise and experience, it also seems to be possible to receive intuitive information from a distant location, referred to as *nonlocal information*, or information that is transcending time, referred to as *transtemporal information*. Unknown to a lot of people, numerous scientific studies have been conducted revealing that it actually is possible to receive sensory information from people over distance, such as in *telepathy*,[36,37] or from distant locations, such as in *remote viewing*.[38–43]

One class of telepathy experiment is the Ganzfeld experiment. In this experiment the test subject is put in a light state of trance and is then instructed to pay attention to subtle sensory impressions. At the same time a sender, placed in a different room, is asked to mentally send a randomly selected image to the receiver. After about 15 to 30 minutes, when the sending phase is over, the receiver is given four images to guess the correct image from.

In a meta-analysis over 25 Ganzfeld experiments, where the design enabled the test subject to guess right in 25 percent of the cases, the overall hit rate was 37 percent.[36] The odds for this to happen by chance is about a trillion to one, clearly showing that there has to exist something else than coincidence that enables the test subjects to perceive the telepathically transferred image. When artistically gifted musicians from the Julliard School in New York City were tested, they were even able to produce a hit rate as remarkable as 75 percent.[44] This result is a clear indication that with the right technique and strategies, it is possible to sharpen the acuity of the intuition.

Besides demonstrating that it is possible for information to be transferred between two minds, as in telepathy, researchers have also discovered that it is possible for an individual to expand one's consciousness to receive information from a distant location, such as in *remote viewing*.[38–43] In a meta-analysis of 653 formal sessions and 126 nonformal sessions of remote viewing, conducted at Princeton University from 1976 to 1999, the overall results gave a significant result with odds against chance of 33 million to one that it was possible for an individual to receive sensory impressions from a distant location.[24,38]

An intriguing aspect of the experiments in remote viewing is that the target site often was randomly chosen *after* conducting the remote viewing session, indicating that the time aspect is not important in order for remote viewing to produce useful results.[38,45] Amazingly enough, that means that is seems to be possible to receive *transtemporal information* in remote viewing, meaning that the information either resides in the past or the future, just as demonstrated when the human autonomic nervous system reacts four to seven seconds ahead of watching an upsetting picture.

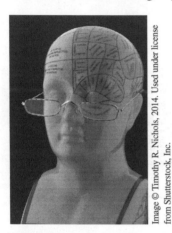

Image © Timothy R. Nichols, 2014. Used under license from Shutterstock, Inc.

Although there exists a vast amount of rigorous experimental research documenting nonlocal and transtemporal intuition,[11–13] most mainstream scientists are either not familiar with these findings, or view them as anomalous.[46] The major reason for this may be that the theoretical knowledge for *how it is possible* is unknown or not that well understood by most people. Therefore, we will review a short summary of how it theoretically is possible to extend one's consciousness outside the traditionally known boundaries of space and time (for a more extensive review see Bradley,[47] Mitchell and Staretz,[48] or Nordstrom[49]).

Quantum Processes Enabling the Reception of Intuitive Data

Although nonlocal and transtemporal intuition seem to contradict the traditional view of how the physical universe operates, three scientific discoveries can assist in better understanding how such phenomena can be possible. The first discovery relates to the verification of **quantum entanglement**,[50] the second concerns *the holographic principle*,[51] and the third is the understanding of *quantum processes occurring in the brain*.[52]

A fascinating aspect of quantum mechanics is that research has discovered that photons, electrons, and groups of molecules can remain in touch even when separated by great distances, a concept called *quantum entanglement*.[50,53,54] That means that particles residing on one side of the planet can be entangled and interconnected with particles on the opposite side of the planet, something Albert Einstein called "spooky actions at a distance."[51]

The existence of entanglement was scientifically proven when two entangled photons, called photon A and B, were sent in two separate directions through 50 km of optical fibers.[50] When each photon arrived to its end station, called Alice and Bob, the entangled property of the sub-atomic particles was affected and then measured (see Figure 6.1). If photon A was spinning in a clockwise direction, the entangled pair, photon B, took on an opposing value, which in this example would be a counter-clockwise spin.

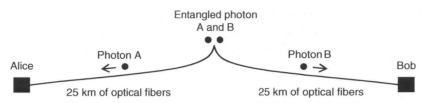

Figure 6.1 Two entangled photons are sent through 50 km of optical fibers.

Quantum physicists believe that quantum entanglement is possible due to the existence of a "hidden" and vast field of energy, referred to as *the zero-point field* (ZPF).[58–56–59] This field consists of massless "virtual particles," such as virtual photons, and is described as ever-present and nonlocal, meaning that it even exists in the empty space of vacuum and in the lowest possible temperature of absolute zero. The ZPF can also store unlimited amounts of information and is described as "nature's information transfer mechanism."[48] This means that everything in the entire universe is interconnected through the medium of the ZPF. However, before understanding how you and I can be interconnected through the ZPF, it is necessary to understand how the ZPF, the brain, and possibly the entire universe process information according to *the holographic principle*.[60–63]

Image © chanpipat, 2014. Used under license from Shutterstock, Inc.

What is a hologram? If you have seen the movie *Star Wars* you probably remember when Luke Skywalker's robot R2D2 projected a holographic image of Princess Leia. The image is three-dimensional and appears in thin air due to the light of two laser beams being used in a particular way. When the hologram is created, a single laser beam is split into two separate beams, beam A and B. While beam A is used to illuminate the recorded object, laser beam B is used as a reference beam. When the illumination beam A hits the object to be photographed, for example Princess Leia, the reflecting waves of light bounce off her and hit a holographic film plate (see Figure 6.2). The waves of light from Princess Leia collide on the holographic film plate with the waves of light from beam B, which creates an interference pattern.

The interference pattern is created when waves of light are colliding and is similar to the wave pattern created when two stones are dropped in a pond of water. When the waves of the two stones are interfering with each other, a crisscross pattern is created. This interference pattern carries the digital information of the object photographed in the form of wavelength, amplitude, and direction—that means that the digital version of Princess Leia actually is stored as an interference pattern on the holographic film plate.

Then, to create a three-dimensional holographic image of the object, a reconstruction beam is beamed at the interference pattern. At the same time as the laser beam is diffracted at the holographic film plate, a three-dimensional holographic image is displayed in the air in front of the observer, just as R2D2 did with Princess Leia. By cutting out a smaller piece of the holographic film plate and beaming a laser beam on the smaller piece, it is still possible to see the entire object. Truly fascinating! However, the more the original plate has been divided, the hazier the image will be. The reason for this is that each

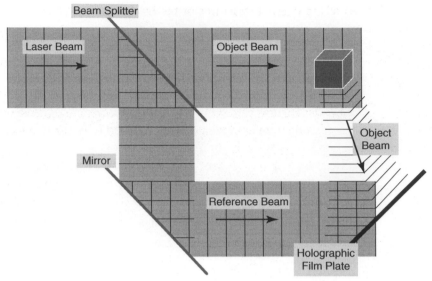

Figure 6.2 The process of recording a hologram.

segment of the interference pattern carries data of the two interfering waves, such as wavelength, amplitude, and direction. That means that each smaller part of the interference pattern also carries information about the whole, which actually also is a quality of the ZPF.

A very interesting idea, that has gained scientific and mathematical support over the past decade, is that the entire universe is constructed in accordance with the holographic principle.[64–66] This idea suggests, "that the whole universe is in some way enfolded in everything and that each thing is enfolded in the whole."[67] For example, Bekenstein[64] has mathematically proven that when energy enters a black hole, it does not disappear into nothingness. Instead, the energy entering the black hole is converted and encoded onto the two-dimensional flat curved surface of the black hole. Bekenstein suggests that the surface of the black hole functions as a holographic film plate, storing the converted energy as an interference pattern of small pixels, having the size of Planck's constant, the smallest measurement known to science.

Other scientists have applied Bekenstein's theory to the entire universe and suggest that even the outer boundaries of the universe is a two-dimensional surface interference pattern, consisting of trillions upon trillions of Planck's constant sized pixels.[66,68] If this is true, one could say that our entire space-time reality is projected into "thin air," similarly to how Luke Skywalker's robot R2D2 projects a holographic image of Princess Leia.

So how does the holographic principle relate to the ZPF? It is suggested that the interconnected aspect of holography is possible due to the ZPF functioning as an interconnecting medium while it is employing the holographic principle. Let us elaborate a little! There exists mounting evidence indicating that every physical object has its own unique "holographic blueprint" stored in the ZPF.[66,69] By using a magnetic resonance imaging (MRI) machine, which uses the holographic principle when it is creating two-dimensional or three-dimensional pictures of the internal structures of the human body, it has been demonstrated that it is possible to decode wave-interference patterns from the ZPF and turn that information into images.[69] What this shows is that objects in the physical reality are represented as quantum information in the ZPF.

Without going into too much detail, it is believed that two entangled objects are interconnected through *resonance* occurring in the ZPF[48]—as an example, if you place two identical guitars on opposite sides of a room and pluck a string on one of them, the same string on the other guitar will begin to vibrate in resonance with the first guitar—then, just as the two guitars are sharing the same standing sound wave, causing them to vibrate in unison, quantum entanglement is believed to occur due to the two objects in resonance are sharing the same standing wave in the ZPF.[48]

With regard to receiving nonlocal and transtemporal information, which is believed to exist as energetic information in the ZPF, various scientists believe that an individual's consciousness can receive such information due to **quantum processes occurring in the brain**.[61,62,70–73] Hameroff,[61,70,71] as well as other scientists[74–76] explain that it is in the microtubules of the dendritic neurons that these quantum operations most likely occur.

These scientists suggest that the microtubules enable the brain to function as a massive quantum computer, "setting up a resonant condition with microtubules scattered throughout the brain tuned to the same frequency as the standing waves of the same frequency located in the ZPF."[48] What does this mean? In the analogy of the two guitars, the brain is one of the guitars vibrating in unison with the energetic imprint of a specific object, individual, memory, or situation in the ZPF. In this sense, the brain uses the microtubules as an interface between the ZPF and the body, accessing data on a quantum level and then converting it into comprehendible information relating to our physical reality.

Thus, nonlocal and transtemporal information is believed to be distributed holographically in the ZPF and can be accessed through a subconscious connection through the ZPF. When this occurs, an outgoing field of attentional energy[77,78] is believed to transcend constraints in time and space and even produce measurable quantum effects at distant locations, just as if our mind on a quantum level can become nonlocally entangled. For example, research has revealed that when remote viewers receive impressions from a target site, they also create a measurable quantum effect at the target site. This effect consists of creating a burst of photons, similar to a miniature camera flash, 100 to 1,000 times above the normal levels of virtual photons already existing in the room[79–81]—this suggests that while the physical body is limited to a certain location in space and time, it seems to be possible for human consciousness to use the holographic principle and the ZPF to move more freely in space and time. The result is that it is possible to "become entangled" to nonlocal and transtemporal information.

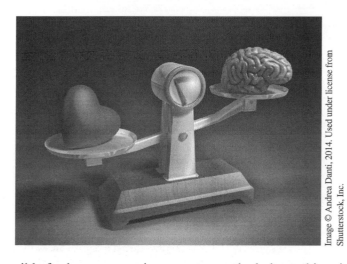

Image © Andrea Danti, 2014. Used under license from Shutterstock, Inc.

Reaching for the Intuitive Genius Within

To conclude this section and get back to something that by now hopefully is a little easier to understand; by using intuition it is possible to *reduce the amount of time to make a decision and still make the decision very sound and accurate*. Research relating to how entrepreneurs, business leaders, pilots, firemen, and military personnel make intuitive decisions even demonstrates that intuitive decisions produce better results compared to when only using analytical and logical reasoning—thus, by building expertise, learning to recognize patterns, and paying full attention to one's intuitive impressions, it is possible to establish a direct connection with one's inner wisdom and make full use of the intuition in one's everyday life.

This is a process that is very similar to how Albert Einstein described how he used intuition to guide him as a scientist. Einstein explained that he very often got scientific ideas from short intuitive insights and that he then used analytical thinking to penetrate deeper into these ideas.[82] Many very successful individuals in the fields of science, business, politics, and sports, have described how they do the same. Some of the most well-known of these "intuitive geniuses" are inventors, such as Leonardo Da Vinci, Thomas Edison, and Nikola Tesla, entrepreneurs and business leaders, such as Richard Branson, Donald Trump, and Steve Jobs, political leaders and freedom fighters, such as Mahatma Gandhi and Nelson Mandela, and sport legends, such as Wayne Gretzky and Michael Jordan.[83,84]

Image © Elena Ray, 2014. Used under license from Shutterstock, Inc.

Although these individuals often relied on their intellect, logic, and reason, the true incentive to their achievement was that they listened to their internal intuitive voice. By paying attention to their intuitive and creative impulses, they excelled in their respective fields and were able to inspire and come up with new ideas that have transformed the world. This connection with our "intuitive genius within" is something that is possible for everyone. You know that experience when you are in the flow, when everything seems to happen naturally and you easily achieve at your best. Most people just happen to end up in this state by coincidence, but they do not really know how to remain there. It turns out that listening to the intuition is the actual key to remain in this state, which is what we will talk more about in the next section.

Let the Magic Begin

In order to make full use of the intuition there are certain skills that the intuitive decisions maker needs to develop. Two fundamentals skills are (1) being able to *quiet and focus the mind* and (2) knowing how to *discern between intuitive impressions and false data*—the reason for this is otherwise it will be difficult to perceive the subtle impressions relating to the intuitive world, as well as to not confuse these intuitive impressions with incorrect "junk data," for instance, relating to unresolved personal issues.

Quieting the Mind and Achieving a High Level of Focus

Before tuning into intuitive information, it is necessary to be able to slow the mind down as well as to mindfully focus on one thing at a time without being disturbed. This relationship between reduced levels of mental noise and increased intuitive abilities is something that has been discovered in individuals that have done yoga and meditation for many years[85,86]—however, it is easier said than done to actually manage to slow the mental stream of the conscious mind down and remain in a quiet state.

Exercise 2—Quieting the Mind

1. Choose a spot on a wall in front of you. Let the spot be slightly above your eye level.

2. Stare at the spot and just let your mind go loose. Eventually, after a minute or two, your focus will spread out and you will gradually begin to see more of the peripheral view.

3. Enter peripheral vision by transferring your focus from the spot to also include everything you can see in your surroundings, as if you are seeing everything at the same time.

4. Every now and then you can close your eyes for a minute or two. Remain in peripheral vision even with your eyes closed. Do your thoughts become more or less active?

One way to gradually develop the ability to quiet the mind is to begin to meditate. Throughout your "Beyond Stress" experience, the Mindful MAC guide meditations give you the opportunity to establish a mindful meditation practice, as well as to begin to use various other tools for living mindfully. There also exist many other forms of meditation that can support quieting the mind. Depending on preference and level of competence, one can use a form of meditation that is either directed externally or internally. In an external meditation, which to most people is easier to perform, the eyes remain open while the practitioner focuses the attention on a specific external object, like a candle, a black dot, or the tip of the nose. In an internal meditation the eyes are closed and the practitioner can, for instance, focus the attention on the natural breath, repeat a word, relax various body parts, or attune to a specific emotion.

Another very efficient way to quiet the mind is to engage the peripheral vision, which is something the ancient shamans of Hawaii, the Kahunas, used to do to cease the mental stream of thoughts and reach a focused state of mind. In Hawaiian this method is called Hakalau, which means, "To stare at, as in meditation and to allow to spread out."[87]

In *exercise two* you can practice quieting your mind by activating your peripheral vision. Since the heart is reacting to intuitive impressions before the brain does,[19] it is advised to bring the awareness into the area of the heart while engaging peripheral vision.

Discerning Between Correct Intuitive Impressions and Incorrect False Data

In order to understand how intuitive data can be distorted, it is helpful to understand that unresolved experiences often influence how an individual makes both conscious and unconscious choices. The reason for this is that unresolved subconscious blockages often direct an individual to avoid the painful and unpleasant aspects of life, relating to the self-preservation instinct, as well as to follow the desire to attract, possess, and experience pleasure in life, associated with the sexual instinct.[88,89]

With regard to using intuition, the process of reacting to unresolved content relating to *fear of anything that can cause pain* and *desire for anything that is pleasurable,* can therefore be said to distract the conscious mind from correctly "hearing," "feeling," or "seeing" the much more subtle intuitive data—in this sense, intuitive expressions are internally "played with a low volume," while subconscious fears and desires can be described, from an auditory perspective, to be very noisy when they become activated, thereby, overtaking the mental stream of consciousness and making the intuitive data appear as faint background noises.

Thus, a key aspect in the mental simulation is to be able to intuitively perceive if the result of the simulation will work or not. In this process it is helpful to become aware of how true intuitive impressions are experienced. A very important aspect to remember here is that true intuitive data not necessarily is the same as a "feeling in the gut," or gut feelings, which also can be related to unresolved emotions, something that will be discussed more in detail further on.

An easy and efficient way to calibrate how true intuitive impressions are experienced is to attune with past situations in which the intuitive guidance turned out to be correct.[49(p.57)] For instance, the sensation of being intuitively *guided to* perform a certain action is often experienced very differently from being *warned about* doing something, similarly as how a word spelled correctly versus an incorrect spelled word is experienced.

As an example, the intuitive "go ahead signal" can feel like a *surge of positive energy* being released in the stomach, slowly moving upwards. The tissue in that particular region of the stomach may *relax* and one may experience *becoming a little warmer*. Different parts of the body *may loosen up* and it is common to feel a sense of *excitement and happiness*. On the other hand, when intuitively sensing that something is wrong, that something will not work, or that one should avoid doing something, the sensation is almost the opposite. For example, the region of the *diaphragm may contract*, as if a small knot the size of a golf ball is located in the solar plexus. It can feel like *being drained of energy* and one might even *become tired*, as if the nervous system is time traveling and experiencing how one would feel in that future scenario.

In *exercise three* you will learn how to calibrate your intuitive "yes" and "no" signal, also referred to as the "go ahead signal" and the "avoid doing signal." The more you continuously practice calibrating and sensing how intuitive impressions are experienced, compared to distorted impressions, the easier it will be to differ between the two.

A key point here is that intuitive impressions, especially concerning a decision that will have a major influence on one's life, almost always will be blended with incorrect "junk data" relating to

---

Exercise 3—The Yes and No Signal

1. Identify two separate events, one when your intuition has been guiding you to *go ahead with something*, such as which direction to take in life, and one event when you have been guided *not to do something*, for instance, being warned about danger or a person. It is important that afterwards it turned out that your intuitive guidance was correct.

2. Close your eyes and think about one of the two intuitive events. Imagine yourself being back in your physical body at the time of the event.

3. Calibrating your intuitive yes and no signal.
   a. How did you experience the sensation of intuitively knowing what to do on a mental, emotional, and physical level?
   b. In which area of your body did you perceive a change? How big is the size of that area? Golf ball? Tennis ball? Put a matching color to that area.

4. Repeat the same process with the remaining event from point 2.

5. Notice the difference in sensation between when the intuition is *guiding* you to do something from when it is *warning* you from doing something.

one's unconscious fears and desires. Some examples of these fears and desires can be a fear of not succeeding, not being good enough, not having enough money, not being liked or accepted, respectively the desire to possess things, the longing to take the easy way out, to wish for things to happen without needing to work for it, or not wanting to take responsibility for ones actions. To make the data "purer," one can either try to deepen one's level of relaxation, or use a therapeutic method for resolving the unprocessed data.

How to Perform the Mental Simulation When Making Intuitive Decisions

When you have calibrated your intuitive "go ahead signal" and "avoid doing signal," the next step is to begin practicing on constructing mental simulations. As discussed earlier, when making a decision or solving a problem, it is necessary to allow for the subconscious "super-computer" to perform pattern recognition, as well as to receive nonlocal and transtemporal information relating to the particular situation.

The following five steps will assist the practitioner in performing the mental simulation: (1) think about the problem at hand, (2) quiet the mind and enter an intuitive reception mode, (3) intuitively come up with suggestive solutions, (4) use felt sense to determine the validity and usability of the received information, and (5) determine and act upon the first intuitively congruent action identified reasonable to act upon (see more Figure 6.3).

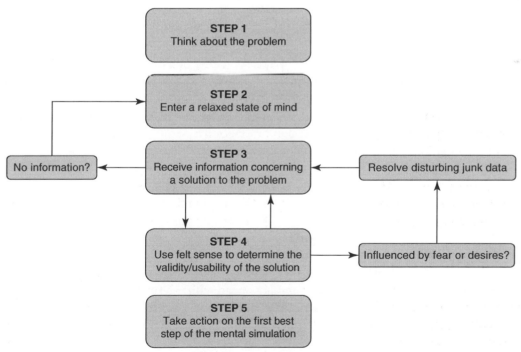

Figure 6.3 A general flowchart of how to perform a mental simulation.

Step 1 is to *think about the problem at hand* and set the intention to receive or discover a solution to the situation. Use an "internal mental screen" to make it easier to picture the situation as vividly as possible, preferably with all your inner senses—for instance, if you are in a situation in which you are having a problem with a friend, use your internal 3D movie screen to imagine that you are seeing the face of your friend, hearing the friend's voice, and sensing that you are physically present with your friend.

In Step 2, enter an *intuitive reception mode,* in which your mind has quieted down substantially, and the intention is set to receive intuitive information. Try to have no expectations since that will distort the intuitive information. Use felt sense while paying attention to any intuitive impressions being conveyed on the physical, mental, emotional, and/or universal/spiritual level. If your analytical mind becomes too active, focus on your breathing until you are back in a receptive mode.

In Step 3, allow for the subconscious "super-computer" *to creatively pop up suggestive solutions.* There is no need to be too serious, too strict, or too exact in this process. Instead a playful and enjoyable state of mind is very much preferred. The reason for this is that otherwise the intuitive information from the subconscious mind will be blocked by the analytical mind. This is similar to as when calling a friend and the person cannot answer because he or she is busy talking to someone else.

In *Step 4* (which often can be done simultaneously as Step 3) use felt sense to determine if the received information is (1) useful, (2) needs to be modified, or (3) cannot be used at all. What does this mean? While part of your awareness is busy constructing a mental simulation on your internal movie screen, another part of your awareness is using felt sense to determine if the different parts of your mental simulation are constructed in accordance with your intuition or not—that means that intuition and your felt sense function as an "internal compass" deciphering if the mental simulation is in alignment with the performed subconscious pattern-recognition and/or the subconsciously perceived nonlocal and transtemporal information.

Until you intuitively perceive that you have reached a valid solution, meaning that your felt sense coincides with your "go ahead signal," you can go back and forth between Steps 3 and 4. Begin by changing the solution you are testing by either (1) breaking the test scenario down into more or less details, (2) modify or replace certain key aspects of the test scenario, or (3) try out a totally new test scenario.

Remember that if you are experiencing conflicting or incongruent feelings while performing the mental simulation, there is probably some sort of unresolved feeling or emotion that covertly is influencing the process. Since any form of fear of experiencing pain and negative emotions, or any kind of desire for experiencing pleasure and positive emotions, will filter the "pure" intuitive information, it is vital to look deeper into these obstructing elements.

The final part of Steps 3 and 4 is to put the information together into several transition points and then use your felt sense to determine a solution for the entire scenario. Here you may use your mental screen to imagine about two to three key events, as if they were played on a movie screen, and then use felt sense to determine if you feel congruent about your mental simulation. As an example, an individual who is deciding whether to move to another city might imagine the following snapshots: (1) selling the apartment, (2) moving into a new apartment in the new city, (3) doing a particular activity in the new city such as working out, meeting friends, or going for a walk.

When felt sense has been used to confirm the scenario presented in the mental simulation, *Step 5* is to determine the first best action to act upon. Remember, that a vital part of expert intuition is to go with the *first identified reasonable action,* meaning going ahead with the first intuitively congruent action. In the example above, the first best possible action can be, for example, to contact a real estate agent or start looking at new apartments in the new city. Once again, felt sense and a mental simulation can be used to determine if the first intuitively presented real estate agent or apartment is the "intuitively smartest" alternative or not.

Exercise 4—The Mental Simulation

1. Think about something you want to make a decision about.

2. Enter an *intuitive reception mode* in which your mind is quiet with the intention of receiving intuitive impressions about possible solutions.

3. Pay attention to and write down the intuitive impressions that you are receiving. Remember that intuitive information often just pops up into your awareness. Stay open to receiving a wide variety of impressions, for instance, images, sounds, smells, knowings, memories, physical sensation and emotional impressions.

4. Receiving more information or if you are not getting any information:
   a. Deepen your level of relaxation by exhaling slowly.
   b. Stay passive by just remaining quiet and waiting for more intuitive information to surface.
   c. Become active by inner dialoguing with your intuitive mind. Ask for something specific that you can hear, feel, see, or sense in any possible way. Remember to remain in a state of non-attachment, meaning that you do not expect the information to come in any specific presupposed way.

5. Use felt sense while imagining suggestive solutions on your mental screen. Continue until you have reached a valid solution, meaning that your felt sense is similar to your "go ahead signal."

6. Go ahead with the first best action to act upon.

   Remember that in the beginning it is easier to practice on decisions that are not that important and does not have a huge impact on your life.

A difficulty in this process is that the novice in using the intuition easily can get trapped in filtering out or not paying attention to the first reasonable option—when that occurs it is common that the analytical mind runs through too many different scenarios, instead of going with the first best option. If that is the case, it often helps to deepen the *intuitive reception mode* by enhancing one's level of relaxation.

Another common experience is that incorrect junk data, originating from obstructing unresolved feelings and emotions, influences the process negatively. When that is the case, it is necessary to resolve these elements. Until a resolution has occurred it is recommended to not make any decision at all. Then, when the issue is resolved, one can start all over again.

Now you can use *exercise four* to begin practicing performing your own mental simulations. It is necessary to remember that without a "sufficient amount of expertise and background knowledge, it may be difficult or impossible to build a mental simulation,"[31] therefore, if you want to begin using your intuition for solving problems and making decisions, it is vital to build expertise in the area you want to be efficient in.

Since this book is about stress management, it is necessary to build more expertise concerning life and oneself. One efficient way to do that is to adapt an approach to life in which you review and recapitulate major experiences in your life and ask yourself questions like, "What have I learned from

this experience?" "What can I do differently if it would happen again?" and "What actions can I take right away to demonstrate that I've learned from this experience?" The rewards of this approach in life can be many, as briefly discussed in the next section.

The Path of Flow and Synchronicity

Here is an interesting observation I have made from counseling clients over the years. The more an individual acts upon intuitive guidance, the more *flow and chance like coincidences* also seem to occur in their life. While psychology professor Mihaly Csikszentmihalyi has studied the sensation of flow in people who spent their time engaged in activities they really enjoyed doing, such as artists, athletes, musicians, chess masters, and surgeons;[90] Swiss psychiatrist Carl Jung has written extensively about the idea that two or more events can be meaningfully related, referred to as *synchronicity*.[91(p.4)]

The state of flow, which is something that everyone experiences from time to time, is by Csikszentmihalyi defined as "the state in which people are so involved in an activity that nothing else seems to matter; the experience itself is so enjoyable that people will do it even at great cost, for the sheer sake of doing it"[90]—this unselfconscious state can also be characterized by being in effortless control, feeling alert and strong, and at the same time performing at the peak of one's ability.

However, a common idea is that it is not possible to experience flow when it comes to performing some of the more mundane tasks of everyday life. Interestingly enough, Italian psychologists have discovered cultures that have evolved in such a way that the inhabitants' everyday working activities clearly resemble flow activities.[90(p.126)] The most noticeable feature of such cultures is that the inhabitants rarely can separate work from spare time, and it can be argued that they either work 16 hours per day or that they never work.

Thus, imagine if one could spend more time in a state of flow, no matter if one is studying, working, or doing any other activity. A key aspect seems to be choosing in accordance with what intuitively feels right, what feels exciting, and gives energy, as well as doing the things that one is curious about, not because someone else thinks I should do something, but because I am really interested in the subject or the particular activity. This is *not choosing out of selfishness, indolence, or laziness*, but rather to do self-inquiry to discover what do I find purpose in and really enjoy doing at the same time.

One of the many difficulties is that it can take a lot of courage to follow one's inner guidance. To do something new when one is afraid of losing something old can be very challenging—however, the more an individual has learned from one's experiences in life and as a consequence gradually improves one's ability to predict various life patterns, the easier it seems to be to trust one's intuitive guidance.

People who choose in accordance with one's inner truth and experience the state of flow for a longer period of time, often report that they experience that events strangely coincide in startling ways. Jung refers to this as synchronicity and describes it as "the occurrence of meaningful coincidences which, in themselves, are chance happenings, but are so improbable that we must assume them to be based on some kind of principle, or on some property of the empirical world."[91]

Jung explains that a synchronistic event consists of two factors: (1) An unconscious image, idea, or insight that has sprung into consciousness, and (2) An objective situation that corresponds to the subjective content. Although often no causal connection can be found between the two parts of a synchronistic event, they are still meaningfully related. Therefore, Jung believed that synchronistic events demonstrate the existence of a larger underlying pattern to how we experience our daily life, similarly to the earlier presented information about quantum processes enabling the reception of intuitive data.

One of the key aspects to experiencing flow and synchronicity seems to be to choose in accordance with one's inner truth and intuitive guidance. Therefore, one may conclude that when you follow your curiosity, excitement, and natural instinct to grow and learn new things, you will experience a natural flow in life, as if you are on the "right track" in life. I refer to this track as the *path of flow and synchronicity* (see Figure 6.4.).

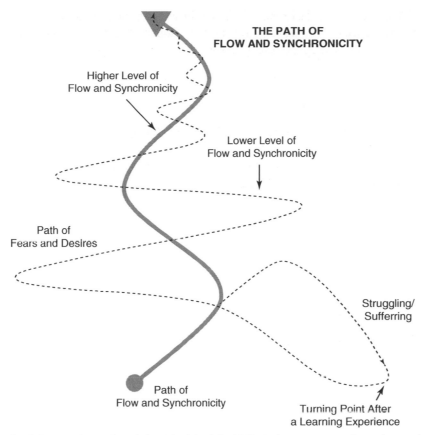

THE PATH OF FLOW AND SYNCHRONICITY

Higher Level of Flow and Synchronicity

Lower Level of Flow and Synchronicity

Path of Fears and Desires

Struggling/ Sufferring

Path of Flow and Synchronicity

Turning Point After a Learning Experience

Figure 6.4 The path of flow and synchronicity (the black bold line) demonstrates that when using the intuition it is common to experience a higher level of flow and synchronicity in one's life. The path of fears and desires (the black dotted line) relates to when our choices are influenced by fears of experiencing pain and/or desires of experiencing pleasure. The *learning experience* either reflects an *inner change* in how one experiences the world, and/or a direct external change of some sort.

Remember, the path of flow and synchronicity is an *ideal model* of the world, not a real model—its purpose is to symbolically demonstrate that when choosing in accordance with intuitive guidance and one's deeper inner truth it is common to experience a higher level of flow and synchronicity—this is in contrary to when an individual has been choosing out of alignment with one's inner truth for too long, which may lead to an experience of the external world as being harsh and difficult to master.

That one's experience is being influenced by fears and desires, which in figure four is symbolized by *the path of fears and desires*, is a natural part of living and something that everyone recognizes. A constructive way to deal with it is to become aware of when it happens and then try to learn from it—that means that when an individual has been struggling, suffering, and experiencing lack of flow for a while, it is often very helpful to learn from the past and make some sort of change in one's life. These changes can either be reflected by an *internal change* of how one experiences the world, or an *external change* of how to go about things in the world, such as changing a behavior, activity, or relation.

As a part of becoming "your own scientist," who tests and examines things in your life and discerns what is your truth and what is the truth of other's, you may ask yourself the following question for the

Exercise 5—The Intuitive Compass

1. When you are about to make a choice, list the different options you can choose from. At least consider three different alternatives.

2. Close your eyes and think about one option at a time.
   a. Imagine yourself being in one of the future alternatives as vividly as possible. Pay attention to how you are reacting on a physical, emotional, and mental level.
   b. Rate and write down your experienced level of excitement/curiosity/energy on a scale from 1 to 10, where 8-10 is very excited (ex. high level of flow), 4-6 is moderate (ex. can do it but not that much flow), and 2-3 not excited at all (ex. loosing energy).
   c. Discern if your "intuitive judgment" has been clouded. *Fears of experiencing pain and negative emotions* may be influencing your rating negatively (ex. you may first feel excited but then you become scared), or *desires of experiencing pleasure and positive emotions* may make your rating too high (ex. wishful thinking/hoping for a change). Change your rating if necessary.
   d. Repeat the above process with your remaining alternatives.

3. If possible choose the option with the highest rating.

next couple of months: *When I act upon my intuition and what feels meaningful to me, do I then more regularly experience flow and synchronicity in my life?* That means that when you are following your curiosity and excitement, no matter whether it relates to the small or the large decisions in life, do you then more often experience being on the right track in life?

Remember, that rather than coming up with the "right answer," the aim is foremost the process of asking the question and *searching* for an answer—in this process you will automatically direct your attention towards observing how you choose in life, and over time hopefully enhance your ability to intuitively perceive the outcome of your choices.

To assist you in finding your own answers to the above question, you can use *exercise five* as a way to discern when you are choosing out of curiosity, excitement, and the natural urge for growing and learning new things, compared to when you are choosing out of old habits and how you *should* do things.

Then, when you have more practical experience of using your intuition consciously, you can determine whether you are able to use the intuition as one of the new strategies for making efficient decisions, tackling information overload, and dealing with the rapid changes of our time, as futurist Toffler discussed back in the 1970s—thus, as suggested in the beginning of this chapter, is it possible that by becoming "intuitively smart," the individual of the twenty-first century will be able to choose smarter, save valuable time, experience more exciting things, develop faster, and get to know the deeper aspects of oneself even more exquisitely. The future will tell! Until then, "Vincit qui se vincit!" (English: "He conquers who conquers himself").

References

1. Dow, R., *Picture Named Monkey Mind*. Accessed March 11, 2014, http://www.talkshoe.com/custom/images/icons/TC-38032-MainIcon.gif Reproduced with permission.
2. Toffler, A., *Future Shock*. Random house. New York, United States of America, 1970.

3. Cohen, S., & Janicki-Deverts, D., "Who's Stressed? Distributions of Psychological Stress in the United States in Probability Samples from 1983, 2006, and 2009," *Journal of Applied Social Psychology* 42 no. (6) (2012): 1320–1334. DOI: 10.1111/j.1559-1816.2012.00900.x.

4. Neal, M., *Stress Levels Soar in America by up to 30% in 30 Years* (Paragraph 15). *New York Daily News*, 2012. Accessed October 8, 2013, http://www.nydailynews.com/news/national/stress-levels-soar-america-30-30-years-article-1.1096918.

5. Speier, C., Valacich, J., & Vessey, I., "The Influence of Task Interruption on Individual Decision Making: An Information Overload Perspective," *Decision Sciences* 30 no. (2) (1999): 337–60.

6. Field Manual 5-0 Army Planning and Orders Production, Headquarters Department of the Army. Washington, DC, January 20, 2005. Accessed November 22, 2013, http://www.usu.edu/armyrotc/Tools/Army%20Planning%20and%20Orders%20Production%20FM%205-0.pdf.

7. Ross, K. G., Klein, G., Thunholm, P., Schmitt, J. F., & Baxter, H. C., "The Recognition-primed Decision Model," *Military Review* 74 no. (4) (2004): 6–10.

8. Thunholm, P., *A New Model for Tactical Mission Planning for the Swedish Armed Forces: Proceedings of the 2006 Command and Control Research and Technology Symposium: The state of the art and the state of the practice.* June 20-22, San Diego, CA. Washington, DC: Command and Control research Program (CCRP), 2006.

9. Klein G., *Expert intuition and naturalistic decision making* (Page 69). Presented in Handbook of Intuition Research, edited by Marta Sinclair, 69-78. Edward Elgar Publishing Limited, Northampton, MA, 2011.

10. Radin D., *The Noetic Universe: The Scientific Evidence for Psychic Phenomena* (Page xiii). London: Transworld Publishers, 2009.

11. Radin D., "Unconscious Perception of Future Emotions: An Experiment in Presentiment," *Journal of Scientific Exploration* 11 (1997):163–80.

12. Bradley R.T. "Psychophysiology of Intuition: A Quantum-holographic Theory of Non-local Communication: World Future," *Journal of General Evolution* 63 no. (2) (2007): 61–97.

13. Bradley, R.T., Gillin, M., McCraty, R. & Atkinson, M., "Nonlocal Intuition in Entrepreneurs and Non-entrepreneurs: Results of Two Experiments Using Electrophysiological Measures," *International Journal of Entrepreneurship and Small Business* 10 (2010):324–48.

14. Spink, A. *Information Behavior: An Evolutionary Instinct* (Page 35). Springer Berlin Heidelberg. Germany, 2010.

15. Merriam-Webster (2013a). Merriam-Webster Online Dictionary. Accessed October 22, 2013, http://www.merriam-webster.com/dictionary/instinct.

16. Sheldrake, R., "Listen to the Animals: Why Did So Many Animals Escape December's Tsunami?," *The Ecologist*, March 2005.

17. Mott, M., "Did Animals Sense Tsunami Was Coming?," *National Geographic News*, January 4, 2005. Accessed October 24, 2013, http://news.nationalgeographic.com/news/2005/01/0104_050104_tsunami_animals_2.html.

18. Bierman D. J., *Anomalous Baseline Effects in Mainstream Emotion Research Using Psychophysiological Variables. Proceedings of Presented Papers: The 43rd Annual Convention of the Parapsychological Association*, 2000:34–47.

19. McCraty, R., Atkinson, M., & Bradley, R., "Electrophysiological Evidence of Intuition: Part 1. The Surprising Role of the Heart," *Journal of Alternative and Complementary Medicine*

10 no. (1) 2004: 133–143. Accessed October 28, 2013, http://www.heartmath.org/templates/ihm/downloads/pdf/research/publications/intuition-part1.pdf.

20. McCraty, R., Atkinson, M., & Bradley, R. T., "Electrophysiological Evidence of Intuition: Part 2. A System-wide Process?," *Journal of Alternative and Complementary Medicine*, 10 no. (2) (2004): 325–36. Accessed October 28, 2013, http://www.heartmath.org/templates/ihm/downloads/pdf/research/publications/intuition-part2.pdf.

21. Radin, D., "Electrodermal Presentiments of Future Emotions," *Journal of Scientific Exploration*, 18 (2004): 253–73.

22. Spottiswoode J., & May E. C., "Skin Conductance Prestimulus Response: Analyses, Artifacts and A Pilot Study," *Journal of Scientific Exploration* 17 (2003): 617–42.

23. Bierman, D. J., & Scholte, H. S., *Anomalous anticipatory response on randomized future exposure of emotional and neutral pictures. Paper presented at the Toward a Science of Consciousness IV conference*, Tucson, AZ, 4-8 April., 2002.

24. Radin, D., *Entangled Minds: Extrasensory Experiences in a Quantum Reality*. Pocket Books, a division of Simon & Schuster, New York, United States of America, 2006.

25. Schmidt, S., Schneider, R., Utts, J., & Walsch, H., "Distant Intentionality and the Feeling of Being Stared at: Two Meta-analyses," *British Journal of Psychology* 95 (2004): 235–47.

26. Sheldrake, R., "The Sense of Being Stared at: Experiments in Schools," *Journal of the Society for Psychical Research* 62 (1998): 311–23.

27. Sheldrake, R., "Sheldrake and His Critics: The Sense of Being Glared At," A special edition of the *Journal of Consciousness Studies* 12 no. (6) (2005).

28. Sheldrake, R., "The Sense of Being Stared At," *Journal of Consciousness Studies* 12 no. (6) (2005): 10–31.

29. Colwell, J., Schröder, S., & Sladen, D., "The Ability to Detect Unseen Staring: A Literature Review and Empirical Tests," *British Journal of Psychology*, 91 (2000): 71–85.

30. Cholle, F. P., (2011). *The Intuitive Compass: Why the Best Decisions Balance Reason and Instinct*" (Paragraph 6). Accessed October 24, 2013, http://www.psychologytoday.com/blog/the-intuitive-compass/201108/what-is-intuition-and-how-do-we-use-it.

31. Klein, G., *Sources of Power: How People Make Decisions*. Cambridge, MA: MIT Press, 1998.

32. Isenberg, D. J., "How Senior Managers Think," *Harvard Business Review* 62 1984: 80–90

33. Green, C., "Nursing Intuition: A Valid Form of Knowledge," *Nursing Philosophy* 13 no. (2) (2012):98–111. doi:10.1111/j.1466-769X.2011.00507.x.

34. Gendlin, E., *Focusing*. New York, NY: Bantam Books, 1982.

35. Vaughan, F., *Awakening Intuition*. New York , NY: Doubleday Dell Publishing Group, 1979.

36. Honorton, C., "Meta-analysis of psi ganzfeld Research: A Response to Hyman," *Journal of Parapsychology* 49 (1985): 51–91.

37. Honorton, C., Berger, R. E., Varvoglis, M. P., Quant, M., Derr, P., Schechter, E. I., & Ferrari, D. C., "Psi communication in the ganzfeld: Experiments With An Automated Testing System and A Comparison With a Meta-analysis of Earlier Studies," *Journal of Parapsychology* 54 (1990): 99–139.

38. Jahn, R. G., & Dunne, B. J., "Information and Uncertainty in Remote Perception Research," *Journal of Scientific Exploration* 17 no. (2) (2003): 207–41.

39. Jahn, R. G., & Dunne, B. J., "The PEAR Proposition," *Journal of Scientific Exploration* 19 no. (2) (2005): 195–245.

40. Puthoff, H. E., "CIA-initiated Vviewing at Stanford Research Institute," *Intelligencer: Journal of U.S. Intelligence Studies*, Summer, 2001: 60–67.

41. Targ, R., "Remote-Viewing Replication: Evaluated by Concept Analysis," *Journal of Parapsychology* 58 (1994): 271–84.

42. Targ, R., *Limitless Mind: A guide to Remote Viewing and Transformation of Consciousness.* Novato, CA: New World Library, 2004.

43. Utts, J. M., *An Assessment of the evidence of psychic functioning.* JSE 10:3-30, 1996. Accessed October 17, 2013, http://www.scientificexploration.org/journal/jse_10_1_utts.pdf.

44. Schlitz, M. J., & Honorton, C., "Ganzfeld psi Performance Within an Artistically Gifted Population," J Am Soc Psych Res 86 (1992): 83–98. Accessed November 20, 2013, http://media.noetic.org/uploads/files/Ganzfeld_Juliard_Study_Journal_of_American_Society_for_Psychical_Research_1992.pdf.

45. Puthoff, H. E., & Targ, R., *A perceptual channel for information transfer over kilometer distances: Historical perspective and recent research.* Proceedings of the IEEE, 64, 1976, 329–354. Accessed November 8, 2013, http://www.lfr.org/lfr/csl/library/IEEE1976.pdf.

46. Walach, H., & Schmidt, S., "Repairing Plato's Life Boat With Ockham's Rrazor: The Important Function of Research in Anomalies for Consciousness Studies," *Journal of Consciousness Studies* 12 no. (2) (2005): 52–70.

47. Bradley, R. T. *The psychophysiology of entrepreneurial intuition: a quantum-holographic theory. Proceedings of the Third AGSE International Entrepreneurship Research Exchange,* February 8–10, 2006, Auckland, New Zealand. Accessed November 7, 2013, http://destinycreatedbyyou.com/linked/bradley_psychophysiology_of_entreprenuerial_intuition.pdf.

48. Mitchell, E., & Staretz, R., "The Quantum Hologram And the Nature of Consciousness," *Journal of Cosmology* 14 (2011). Accessed April 1, 2014, http://journalofcosmology.com/Consciousness149.html.

49. Nordstrom, J., *Medical Intuition: The Science of Intuitively Perceiving Physical Ailments and Diseases.* Kona University, Hawaii. Retrieved November 20, 2013, http://www.minskadinstress.se/storage/Jonas_Nordstrom%20Dissertation%20Medical%20Intuition.pdf.

50. Marcikic, I., de Riedmatten, H., Tittel, W., Zbinden, H., Legré, M., & Gisin, N., *Distribution of Time-Bin Entangled Qubits over 50 km of Optical Fiber. Physical Review Letters* 93 no. (18) (2004).

51. Gabor, D., *1900-1979. Nature* 280 (5721) (1979): 431–33.

52. Jibu, M., Hagan, S., Hameroff, S. R., Pribram, K. H., & Yasue, K., "Quantum Optical Coherence in Cytoskeletal Microtubules: Implications for Brain Function," *Biosystems* 32 no. (3) (1994):195–209.

53. Bell, J., "On the Einstein Podolsky Rosen Paradox," *Physical Review* 1 no. (3) (1964): 195–200.

54. Bohm, D. J., & Hiley, B. J., "On the Intuitive Understanding of Nonlocality as Implied by Quantum Theory," *Foundations of Physics* 5 no. (1) (1975): 99–109.

55. Born, M., & Einstein, A., *The Born-Einstein Letters: Friendship, Politics and Physics in Uncertain Times* (Page 155). New York: Macmillan, 2005.

56. Bressi, G., Carugno, G., Onofrio, R., & Ruoso, G., "Measurement of the Casimir Force between Parallel Metallic Surfaces," *Physical Review Letters* 88 no. (4) (2002): 041804.

57. Heisenberg, W., *The Physical Principles of the Quantum Theory.* New York, NY: Courier Dover Publications, 1949.

58. Laidler, K. J., *The World of Physical Chemistry.* Oxford University Press, Oxford, 2001.

59. Lamoreaux, S., *Demonstration of the Casimir Force in the 0.6 to 6 µm Range. Physical Review Letters* 78 (1997): 5.

60. Bohm (1980; 1990)

61. Hameroff, S., "How Quantum Brain Biology Can Rescue Conscious Free Will," *Frontiers in Integrative Neuroscience* 6 (2012):93. doi:10.3389/fnint.2012.00093. Epub 2012 Oct 12.

62. Pribram, K., *Brain and Perception: Holonomy and Structure in Figural Processing.* Hillsdale, NJ: Lawrence Erlbaum Associates, 1991.

63. Penrose, R., *Shadows of the Mind: A Search for the Missing Science of Consciousness.* Oxford: Oxford University Press, 1994.

64. Bekenstein, J. D., *Information in the Holographic Universe.* Scientific American, August, 2003:59–65.

65. Hogan, C., *The Online Archive of Craig Hogan's 82 Scientific Articles.* Cornell University Library, 2013. Accessed October 28, 2013, http://arxiv.org/find/astro-ph/1/au:+Hogan_C/0/1/0/all/0/1.

66. Susskind, L., "The World as a Hologram," *Journal of Mathematical Physics* 36 no. (11) (1995): 6377–96.

67. Bohm, D., *A new theory of the relationship of mind and matter* (Page 2). *Philosophical Psychology* 3, no. 2 (1990): 271–86. See also http://evans-experientialism.freewebspace.com/bohmphysics.htm.

68. Hooft, G., *Dimensional Reduction in Quantum Gravity,* 1993, 10026. eprint arXiv:gr-qc/9310026. Accessed May 15, 2013 from http://arxiv.org/abs/gr-qc/9310026.

69. Schempp, W., *Magnetic Resonance Imaging: Mathematical Foundations and Applications.* Canada: Wiley-Liss, 1998.

70. Hameroff, S., *Ultimate Computing: Biomolecular Consciousness and NanoTechnology.* AZ: Elsevier Science Publishers B.V., 1987.

71. Hameroff, S., "Consciousness, Neurobiology and Quantum Mechanics: The Case for a Connection". In *The Emerging Physics of Consciousness*, edited by Jack Tuszynski, Springer-Verlag, 2007.

72. Tiller, W., *Some Science Adventures with Real Magic.* Walnut Creek: Pavior Publishing, , California, 2005.

73. Tiller, W., *Psychoenergetic Science: A Second Copernican-Scale Revolution.* Walnut Creek, CA: Pavior Publishing, 2007.

74. Jibu, M., & Yasue, K., *A Physical Picture of Umezawa's Quantum Brain Dynamics.* In Cybernetics and Systems Research, edited by Trappl, R. World Scientific, 1992.

75. Jibu, M., & Yasue, K., *Introduction to Quantum Brain Dynamics.* In *Nature, Cognition and System*, Carvallo: M. Kluwer Academic, 1993.

76. Jibu, M & Yasue, K., "Intracellular Quantum Signal Transfer". *Cybernetics and Systems* 24 (1993): 1–7.

77. Marcer, P., "A Proposal for Mathematical Specification for Evolution and the Psi Field," *World futures: The Journal of General Evolution* 44 no. (283) (1995): 149–59.

78. Marcer, P., & Schempp, W., "Model of the Neuron Working by Quantum Holography," *Informatica* 21 (1997): 519–34.

79. Hubbard, G. Scott, May, E.C., & Puthoff, H. E., *"Possible Production of Photons During a Remote Viewing Task: Preliminary Results. SRI International"*. In *Research in Parapsychology* 1985 edited by D.H. Weiner & D.I. Radin, 66–70. Metuchen, NJ: Scarecrow Press, 1986.

80. Yonjie, Zhao & Hongzhang, Xu., *EHBF Radiation: Special Features of the Time Response.* Institute of High Energy Physics, Beijing, China, PSI Research, December, 1982.

81. PRC, Chinese Academy of Science, *Exceptional Human Body Radiation.* High Energy Institute, Special Physics Research Team. Psi Research, June, 1982, 16–25.

82. Hermanns, W., *Einstein and the Poet: In Search of the Cosmic Man.* Branden Press. Brookline Village, MA, 1983.

83. Lodovico, G. J., *The Genius Code: The Twelve Pillars of Creative Geniuses.* iUniverse. Bloomington, IN, 2008.

84. Mills, K.L., *Invisible Genius: The Intuition Secrets of the World's Greatest Leaders and How to Profit From Them.* Imaginicity Pty Ltd. Buderim, Australia, 2012.

85. Braud, W. G., & Braud, L. W., *Preliminary Exploration of psi-conducive States: Progressive Muscular Relaxation. JASPR* 67 (1973):27–46.

86. Honorton, C., Psi and Internal Attention States". In Handbook of parapsychology, edited by B.B. Wolman, 435-72, New York, NY: Van Nostrand Reinhold, 1977.

87. James, T., *Lost Secrets of Ancient Hawaiian Huna, vol 1* (Page 33). Honolulu: Ka Ha O Hawai'I Foundation, 1997.

88. Fortune, D., *The Esoteric Philosophy of Love and Marriage.* York Beach: Samuel Weiser Inc, 2000.

89. Fortune, D., *Psychic Self-Defense.* York Beach: Red Wheel/Weiser, 2001.

90. Csikszentmihalyi, M., *Flow: The Psychology of Optimal Experience.* New York: Harper & Row, 1990.

91. Jung, C. G., [1952]. *Synchronicity: An Acausal Connecting Principle* (From: The Collected Works of C. G. Jung Vol. 8 Bollingen Series XX). Bollingen, Switzerland: Bollingen Foundation, 1993.

Name: _____   Date: _____

Quiz questions related to Chapter Six:

1. Describe the concept of Intuitive Smartness discussed in this chapter.

2. How is a hologram created and what specifically is it that enables one piece of an interference pattern to contain information about the whole?

3. What are the suggested functions of the zero-point field (ZPF) in relation to perceiving nonlocal and transtemporal information?

4. Describe what "a felt sense" means.

5. Have you ever experienced that your instincts have warned you of danger? Elaborate and discuss with a friend.

6. How does paying attention to instinct help one in making better decisions?

7. How does quieting the mind foster increased access to information from your instincts?

8. What are the major differences between instinct and intuition?

9. How can your intuition be used to determine what and when to eat, drink, and rest?

10. What does the concept of "flow" mean?

11. Discuss the concept of synchronicity.

12. What can you do when you are experiencing a lack of flow and synchronicity in your life?

MINDFUL AWARENESS REFLECTION JOURNAL

4 Step **MAC** Guide

Choose one mindful experience as you begin your reflection.

Empathically Acknowledge

Describe your experience

_____

_____

_____

Intentional Attention

Describe what you noticed

Breath
Body
Emotions
Thoughts
Senses

Accept Without Judgment

Describe judgment; acceptance

_____

_____

_____

Willingly Choose

Intention/willingness; new perspective

_____

_____

_____

Mindful Mac Meditation

Describe your meditation experiences. What did you learn?

_____

_____

_____

CHAPTER CRITICAL THINKING AND ACTIVITY JOURNAL

This is an opportunity for you to fully describe your thoughts, opinions and experience following the reading and activities.

The most important information/key concepts we need to understand from these chapters are:

_____

_____

_____

_____

How can I use the information in the chapters to help me with my daily mindfulness practice?

_____

_____

_____

_____

In what ways will the material learned in these chapters help me manage my stress more effectively?

_____

_____

_____

_____

What are your thoughts and feedback regarding the information and activities for each chapter?

_____

_____

_____

_____

CONNECTION TO ALL LIVING THINGS
The Beauty of Relationships
By Bhupin Butaney and Samuel Chates

Photograph courtesy of Maria Napoli

"A human being is a part of the whole world, called by us "Universe," a part limited in time and space. He experiences himself, his thoughts and feelings as something separate from the rest—a kind of optical delusion of his consciousness."

Albert Einstein[1]

If we were to look through a lens that allowed us to view the world on a subatomic level, we would see a world in which all particles (e.g., electrons and protons) were independent, yet held in close proximity to other particles through an invisible force best described as an attraction. This, perhaps, is where the phrase we sometimes use to describe human relationships, "opposites attract," comes from. What we would also see through this special lens is that there are no separations or boundaries among people or objects in the universe. In essence, we perceive separateness and otherness when in fact such distinctions do not actually exist. This idea is so counter to our basic assumptions of self and others that comprehending it can be extremely challenging, let alone assimilating this understanding into our everyday behaviors and activities. The misperception of separateness between self and others underlies the concept of mindfulness, which promulgates a worldview of accepting things as they are and not necessarily as we perceive them to be.

Photograph courtesy of Maria Napoli.

A more common analogy used to explicate this allusive concept is that of a *wave* washing to shore. To the observer, a wave appears to have shape and substance and actually moves toward us. After all, we see this as being so and thus our mind believes the wave to exist. In actuality, not one water molecule in the wave ever moves from its natural location to the shore; water waves visually appear to move over horizontal distances, but the water molecules actually move in a circular pattern with a diameter equal to the wave height. The water particles, thus, return to approximately the same position from which they started. What really travels is the energy transferred by the wind to the water particles that in turn transfers this energy to adjacent water particles.

Image © Aleksandr Sulga, 2014. Used under license from Shutterstock, Inc.

In essence, it is energy that *moves* through it which cannot be perceived by sight.

Another example capturing this seeming paradox between what we observe or perceive and what we know as actually happening is the phenomena known to most of us as *The Wave*, a ritual that takes place in football stadiums across the country. To an observer, it appears that a wave of hands is moving around the stadium, yet not one individual hand is moving except up and back to rest again. The implications for us as human beings living in a world of relationships is that though we may appear separate and distinct, we are ultimately interconnected and our interconnection plays a larger role in the manifestation of events. Each of us through our intentions and actions influence the people around us (flow of energy). In addition to the awareness that we are all interconnected, the aforementioned paradox implies that we may be led astray if we over identify or focus on our perceptions or feelings. Feelings, beliefs, and awareness, itself, of self, and others are not static but simply flow through us moment-to-moment and sometimes into others. Too often we hold on to past feelings or beliefs of who we are or need to be, as if they *belong* to *us*.

The fact that moment-to-moment experiences are distinct and new, allows for hope that things can be different if the past moment was experienced as negative; it also can bring fear and uncertainty if the feelings and beliefs of self and others from the past were experienced as positive. Holding onto past moments or anticipated (future) moments or avoiding present moments because it brings a negative experience leads to disconnection. We are not present in the moment and without being present in the moment we are not in relation to others or to ourselves. Ultimately we suffer because moments are ever changing and bring disappointment that some positive moment is lost and anxiety or fear that some negative moment is upon us and will remain. One possible solution is to allow moments to be as they are and accept them as an ever-flowing chain of positive and negative moments. The capacity to accept moments as they are eliminates the human experience of disappointment or fear within a paradoxical world.

Accepting this perspective may be difficult, but the goal of this chapter is to understand how this view, which we will call *Mindfulness*, offers a perspective that permits us to remain connected to others and the world, despite moments which may arise that hinder our capacity to stay connected in healthy ways to others and to ourselves (i.e., being aware of our immediate experiences, feelings, and thoughts).

The Dilemma of Human Relations

Psychology in the West is grounded in the notion of a healthy normality and state of happiness. We operate with an underlying belief that humans are inherently healthy. With a healthy environment, lifestyle, and opportunities for self-actualization, we believe that we can be happy and content[2]—yet, prevalence studies suggest that approximately 30 percent of the adult population will suffer from a psychiatric disorder at some point in their lifetime.[3] In any given week, ten percent of the population suffers from clinical depression[4,5] and nearly 25 percent of individuals will at some point in their life suffer from substance or alcohol addiction.[6] Recent studies have identified new ailments growing in prevalence such as sex addiction and internet addiction. In addition to traditional psychological problems, individuals universally suffer at different times from feelings of loneliness, racism, physical pain, divorce, death of loved ones, domestic violence, and social alienation. The list seems endless as we can safely conclude that inherent to *being* is *suffering*.

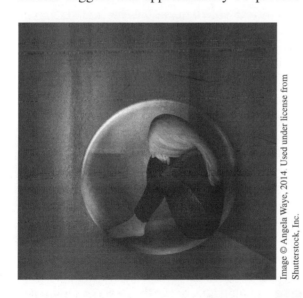

Image © Angela Waye, 2014. Used under license from Shutterstock, Inc.

Many a philosopher has pondered the inherent paradox of living and being. Why should we live in a world that brings such suffering? Writers such has Sartre[7] and Camus[8] have positioned this existential question as the *absurdity* inherent in living, to live in a world without inherent meaning or purpose. After all, what purpose or meaning can there be if after all our efforts, we are to die? Another way to state this dilemma is within a relational context: why should we bother to connect with others, to be in relationship with others, if we will ultimately be disappointed, suffer, and hurt the ones we love? Is it truly the case, as Tennyson[9] puts it, "'Tis better to have loved and lost than to never have loved at all?"

From birth, we have a deep and significant need for others. An infant's initial state or experience in the world is one of helplessness. Dependence on others for satisfaction of all basic needs is a fundamental and universal, early experience. Early theorists believed that it is through our biological needs that we

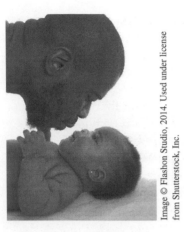

first come to relate to the world and others. We experience somatic tension (e.g., hunger pains) and someone or something in the world gratifies this need. Gratification of this need allows for a return of biologic homeostasis, an internal state experience in which there is no somatic tension. We begin to associate this gratification and reduction in somatic tension, which we can call *pleasure*, with the other or object that brings this gratification or release of tension.

As an infant, gratification is fairly easy to provide. As the infant begins to grow and her/his capacities mature, the infant will come to experience increasing frustrations. The caretaker will not be able to satisfy completely every whim of the growing child. The demands of reality and the world will soon begin to press upon the child and he/she will require his/her caretakers to help mitigate this impact, soothe the child with positive, empathic words when another child is playing on the swing that he or she wishes to play on. These partial gratifications, tension-reducing interactions, serve to strengthen the emotional bond between the child and others, which may have been initially founded on dependence. To cope with the absence of the caretaker or significant others, the child, once acquiring the capacity for object constancy, internalizes representations of significant others to avoid experiencing the absence of significant others—by taking in others we hold on to them to maintain a kind of homeostasis. It is more dynamic because we also internalize the relational patterns or experiences with the other. For instance, children will begin to self-soothe as their parents have done for them. Unfortunately, we hold on to the negative qualities as well, such as the criticism of others in the form of self-criticism, an internalized version of the critical other. As we enter new relationships we tend to project these expectations onto others, how we expect them to be, to regain the lost relationship to others who brought gratification and from whom we learned to love and even hate.

Object relations theorists such as Bowlby[11] have argued that our need to bond to others is even more central and fundamental. These theorists state that our basic need is not physiological but rather relational. We *need* to connect to others; we are wired to search out and be with others. A classic study conducted by Harlow,[12] which has come to be known as the *Wire Mother Experiment*, supports the importance of human contact and connection over basic biologic needs. In his famous study with rhesus monkeys, Harlow found that even though the wire mothers had the food, the baby monkeys preferred the soft cloth mother because of the comfort contact provided. After World War II, infants separated from their families were housed in hospitals where they were kept in cribs and provided for in terms of all their biologic needs. According to Spitz,[13] over a third of these infants failed to survive. From this came the term, *failure to thrive*. In essence, without human contact and relationship, infants struggle to live. These findings suggest that physiological needs may be necessary to the survival of individuals but not sufficient. Human relationships are integral for people to thrive.

Freud,[14] in *Civilization and its Discontents*, explains a life long conflict at the heart of the human condition. Gratification of our basic needs or impulses will sometimes be in conflict with our need to remain connected to others. Society teaches us through its rules that we forgo our personal desires and impulses at times to remain connected to others. Acting on personal impulses or expressing feelings or thoughts may jeopardize relationships with others. Perhaps the most common example of this dilemma is between a child who may be physically or emotionally abused by a parent, a parent whom the child also needs because to be without a parent can feel unfathomable and alarming; a subjective experience of nonexistence. Most likely, the abusive parent may also be supportive and protective at times. Prohibiting personal gratification of impulses for the benefit of maintaining connection results in an experience of discontent or suffering; it becomes the cost of maintaining ties to a social world. Thus one of the greatest challenges or problems we face in life is how do we stay connected to others when we know that such connections also bring pain and disappointment?

Mindfulness and Relationships

Image © Thomas M Perkins, 2014. Used under license from Shutterstock, Inc.

There is strong empirical evidence linking quality and quantity of social relationships with various positive health outcomes.[15,16] Holt-Lunstad, Smith, and Layton[17] examined 148 empirical studies through a meta-analysis and found that social support was related to a 50 percent reduction in risk of future mortality. Social negativity and social support have been found to impact immune system mediated processes.[18] Uchino et al.[19] linked ambivalent relationships, when interactions are both positive and negative, to lower telomeres, structures at the end of chromosomes that help promote cellular stability; shorter telomeres are associated with greater mortality risk for various diseases.[20]

Being in intimate relationships involve exposure at times to strong emotional experiences that include hurt, fear, sadness, anger, jealously, loneliness, and love—having these experiences do not by themselves negatively impact relationship health, but rather how we respond when experiencing these emotions impacts relationship adjustment, intimacy, and satisfaction. Cordova et al.[21] identified several emotion skills essential to marital adjustment and satisfaction. These skills involve the capacity to identify and

communicate emotions, an ability to provide empathy and understanding, and to cope with self and partner emotions. Wachs and Cordova[22] examined the relationship between mindfulness, emotional skills, and marital adjustment. They found that mindfulness decreased anger reactivity and increased ability to identify and communicate negative emotions, which in turn increased marital adjustment.

Mindfulness can be defined as paying attention with flexibility, openness, and curiosity; this implies a nonjudgmental, nonreactive stance toward moment-to-moment events and experiences. Developing the capacity for mindfulness, a capacity to attend and not react despite our natural tendency, allows us to remain present despite our inclination to escape knowing what is happening or what we are feeling in a given moment. Over time, this capacity to stay with feelings, sensations, images, and thoughts leads to greater tolerance of negative emotions. This tolerance is also achieved through a distancing and accepting of the emotion. By nature, individuals avoid negative emotions because we are taught to avoid unpleasant or painful feelings, which we view as threatening happiness and self-integrity. We employ various defensive strategies that are self-deceptive and destructive to escape feeling negative emotions.[23] Mindfulness promotes acceptance and the ability to tolerate all emotions including negative ones. This condition of acceptance, non reactivity, and tolerance provide the context within relationships to inhibit impulsive reacting (e.g., expression of blame or anger) and take in all aspects of the experience such as personal hurt as well as the other's hurt and accept the difference in perspectives. Having access to all aspects of the present moment allow for appropriate and effective responding. By not responding defensively, greater capacity for empathy is available that might engender more supportive responses to conflicts within relationships.

What Hinders Us

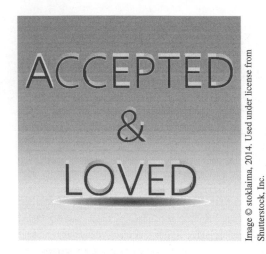

Image © stoklaima, 2014. Used under license from Shutterstock, Inc.

Mindfulness may best be viewed as having a particular type of mental discipline—a focused, flexible attention, and awareness in moment-to-moment experiences. Sustaining such a mental discipline is not easy, especially in the face of intense emotions or unexpected events. Mindful Meditation (MM) is the practice of developing this focus and discipline. One sits in silence and focuses one's mental awareness on an object or process (e.g., breath or breathing) as long as it is present in the moment. No thought, image, or sensation is considered intrusive. One is instructed to accept and acknowledge these distractions and bring one's attention back to the object or process of focus, and not judge or think about it (i.e., analysis or judgment). Over time, one develops the capacity to maintain focus on the present and acknowledge thoughts, images, and sensations without becoming enmeshed with them, confusing them to *be* who we are. The practice of MM has been found to have positive effects on the immune system,[24] to protect against cognitive declines associated with age,[25] and to reduce effectively substance and alcohol addiction.[26] Cerebral areas and sub-cortical structures involved in attentional processes become thicker,[27] implying that neurobiological changes occur through the practice of mindfulness meditation and that these changes remain once acquired.

There are five distinct types of distraction that can hinder our progress toward this type of mental discipline. The first of these is sensory desire, pleasure seeking through the five senses, which distracts us from being present and aware in the moment. When we feel sad, for example, we may turn to a doughnut or listen to upbeat music to "get us out of our funk." This form of coping allows us not to pay attention

Image © kaczor58, 2014. Used under license from Shutterstock, Inc.

to what is actually happening in the present moment. We become oblivious and unaware (at least in terms of conscious processes) of our present experiences. We yearn for the moment before the sadness, perhaps when we believe that we were happier (past), or for some imagined fantasy of what could come to be (future). The cost for this type of coping with an intolerable mental state or emotion is holes in our subjectivity, the chain of subjective experiences in which we perceive our thoughts and feelings within a situation and those of others. Having access to these moment-to-moment experiences creates continuity of experience and a connection to others and the world, connection with *the flow of things*. When we remove ourselves from this process by *not knowing*, we serve to disconnect ourselves, losing experiences of intimacy and connection to others and to the world. Thus, the irony is that by following a path guided by our senses, we move further away from truly connecting, the subjective experience of *being*. Such self-experiences are important in countering the experience of suffering as outlined above by the existentialists.

Translated within the context of relationships, individuals may seek affairs or may become preoccupied by the sensual aspects of a relationship instead of being in the moment and attuned and knowing ones partner fully. Knowing fully allows for the experience of connection, whereas partial knowing leads to partial, fragmented experiences of *being*. This process of relating is similar to what self-psychologists call *self-object relationships*. In these relationships we see only part aspects of others, those parts that are salient to us based on what is missing within ourselves. We relate to others to the extent that they satisfy a self- need. An example of this would be the father who sees his son as a narcissistic extension of himself, recognizing his son's ambitions in football because the father's own ambition was cut short in high school by a career ending injury. It is the father's lost and unfulfilled ambition, in essence, embodied in his perception of his son to whom he relates. What are not recognized are the needs of his son (his genuine thoughts, feelings, and all of his ambitions). Not only is the father stuck in the past (the lost opportunity and his inability to accept that it will not happen), he cannot relate or know his son as his son exists in the present, thus losing the opportunity to truly connect and know his son, another loss. Additionally, the father creates a subjective experience for his son of absence and disconnection with his father (not recognizing the son's *authentic self*). The son may yearn for approval or recognition in the areas that his father has made contingent for

Image © Agnes Kantaruk, 2014. Used under license from Shutterstock, Inc.

his approval and attention to achieve these partial moments of connection. In essence, the son learns to *crave* what can never be truly obtained; thus, the son experiences suffering and struggles to stay present or mindful of himself. In this way, our actions and intention toward the other can set in motion a wave of energy that transfers from one person to another and so on until it reaches some distant shore, generations away.

A second factor that makes it particularly difficult for us to sustain mindful awareness is *ill-will*. Often underlying *ill-will* is resentment or envy toward some quality another possesses or that the individual desperately wishes to attain but believes is unattainable. The consequence is an experienced state of deprivation, not having what one perceives they need (*craving*). *Craving* distracts us from maintaining a stance of mindfulness. Take for example a married couple where the husband has worked hard to reach a point in his business where others run the day-today operations for him. This frees up time for the husband to pursue personal interests and goals (e.g., competitive golf). His wife, who has also worked hard at developing her professional career, continues to work very long hours. Despite being able to cognitively acknowledge her husband's good fortune and circumstances, she is consumed by thoughts and feelings of resentment toward his personal pursuits and expresses this *ill-will* through her actions and communications—such thoughts and actions do not allow her *to be* with her husband in moments. This disconnection may be experienced by her husband as unsupportive and cause him to view the relationship as a source of stress, impinging on his personal goals and happiness. Her husband, subsequently, may be less likely to remain present, himself, in moments with his wife. Underlying this impasse is the inability to accept that people and situations are ever-changing; we suffer when we want impermanent situations to remain and refuse to accept situations as they are in the present. In essence, his wife relates to a version of her husband in the past as constructed by the needs and

Image © Alexander Raths, 2014. Used under license from Shutterstock, Inc.

wishes of his wife. We want people to remain as we need them to be rather than accepting them as they are, remaining curious about them and who they are every moment as they change. Clearly this type of attitude, which we might call *Mindfulness*, is very challenging to maintain; yet, imagine the possibility if such an attitude and stance, to sustain this level of curiosity and acceptance, could be maintained in each moment within relationships.

A *restless mind* is another state of mind that hinders mindfulness. Guilt, anxiety, or regret equate to a mind focused on some past event, preventing connection in the here-and-now moment, an opportunity lost in which a new way of relating may have been experienced. By focusing on past events, we relate to the person in the here-and-now *as if* we were in the past, imbuing him or her with circumstance from "not now," trying to relive or fix something in the past, instead of creating a new, unique experience with the individual before him or her now. Projecting circumstances from the past onto current circumstances reflects our hope for past outcomes to be different, either the outcome never occurring or it being replaced by a desired outcome. As discussed earlier, this process is rooted in early childhood processes of adaption and loss. With the onset of object constancy, we internalize representations of significant others to remain connected to others in their absence. These representations we internalize are then used to imbue new, unknown people (objects), with those qualities, intentions, and powers that past individuals had for us to remain connected to the past individuals though here-and-now relationships and connections.

I treated a 15-year old adolescent boy who was engaged in the developmental process of separation and identity formation. His father had separated from his mother and the adolescent boy was caught in the middle of his parents' divorce. There was quite a bit of anger and hostility between the mother and the adolescent, and the mother found ways to intrude upon her son's sessions. The adolescent welcomed his mother into his sessions and the treatment resembled much of the work done in couples' treatment with communication and empathic understanding being the primary target of treatment. What the mother came to understand through the course of treatment was how she saw her son, who naturally had some features of his father, as if her son *were* his father. The extent of her anger and the issues about which she would become very upset were the same issues and feelings she harbored toward her separated husband. She could not control her husband who had separated from her, but still had control over her son who, too, was in the process of separating from her. From her son's perspective, his mother's attitude could

Image © Sanzhar Murzin, 2014. Used under license from Shutterstock, Inc.

only be internalized as something wrong with his culturally sanctioned desire and goal of separating. His reaction of anger toward his mother fueled his mother's belief that her son needed medications to control his unfounded anger toward her. The mother's anxiety about the end of her marriage and the loss of her partner and more importantly her unresolved anger toward her husband (and inability to have mindful tolerance of such negative affect) resulted in what could be equated to as soul murder toward her son. The damage to her son through this internalization of how his mother feels about him and him becoming a man will carry over to his actions, choices, and his relationship to others including perhaps his own children or spouse. Thus, ignorance begets negative energy, which flows much like the invisible energy responsible for the illusion of the *wave* coming to shore.

Another challenge to maintaining a mindful mind is *laziness* and a *lack of will*. Extreme feelings of disappointment and frustration destroy hope that current interactions can offer gratification. When in this state of mind, individuals retreat from the present moment into their fantasy world where they seek gratification through imagination (e.g., books such as *Harry Potter* or movies like *Lord of the Rings*). Even when the present moment offers gratification, these individuals will often run from the moment because this gratification serves to awaken such intense desire and yearning that intense anger ensues because *past* moments could have been gratifying but were not. The solution becomes the killing of *will* altogether, remaining in a world of thoughts, planning, procrastination, and imaginary permutations of outcomes.

Image © CREATISTA, 2014. Used under license from Shutterstock, Inc.

Doubt and low self-confidence serve as a fifth hindrance to maintaining mindful presence. If past voices of important others have been overly critical, we internalize these other-appraisals as self-appraisals. We identify with (attach) these self-appraisals and they serve as stable ways of seeing *ourselves* as inept, not living up to the expectations of others or oneself. We act *as if* future action may also disappoint, causing us to have doubts. Doubts lead to a lack of faith and commitment. They prevent us from taking chances, to believe that being mindful can free us from suffering or that someone we want to be with the rest of our lives will truly accept us or want to be with us. Within a relational context, doubt moves us away from moments of connection, when, for instance, doubt exists about whether marriage can lead to positive outcomes.

What to do About Hindrances?

Each hindrance impedes adoption of the mindful way, accepting and experiencing what the current moment has to offer, good or bad. The way to handle these hindrances is to first identify and acknowledge that one is desiring, harboring ill-will, experiencing remorse or regret, seeking refuge in inaction, or imbued with doubts. Once recognizing this, we can accept and choose not to condemn ourselves as if this *should not* happen. One should instead accept and become curious about ones state of mind, and investigate it from a number of vantage points. While in this state of mind, notice how it feels in the body, for example, to harbor ill-will. Where in the body does ill-will manifest *physically* (e.g., in the chest or gut or in the temples)? *Emotionally*, does ill-will feel pleasant or unpleasant? Does it change? What is ones' *energy* when experiencing ill-will? Does it increase or decrease? Do you feel pressured and rushed? Excited? Low and depressed? *Cognitively*, what internal narrative does ill-will engender about yourself and others? Do you feel impelled to act or respond in a certain way or to hold onto an idea or someone?

Once one has fully examined the hindrance, one will often notice that the state of mind or feeling fades. Being aware of this process reminds us that this state of mind or inner experience does not define us but pass through like all other thoughts and feelings. We come to accept that this and other experiences come and go, flowing with time, and do not define who we are or forever will be (e.g., the self). If there is one certainty in life, it is that no matter what we feel, experience, believe, or understand in the moment, it will change with time and not remain the same. Someone in the throes of depression will not feel this painful moment every moment of every day for the remaining years of his or her life. Each of us has questioned the meaning and purpose of our life at some point, felt hopeless and depressed; yet, each of us has also experienced joy, happiness, and hope in some subsequent moment. Understanding and accepting this flow of experience as essential to the nature of being is central to the mindful perspective.

As in the example at the onset of the chapter in which none of the water molecules ever moves toward the shore, none of our past events or interactions are actually with us in the current moment, nor will they be with us at our end. The perception of the wave moving to shore is an illusion as is the notion that we are a self and destined to act or respond in a certain manner, a slave to circumstance and suffering. Rather than hold onto past moments in the present, we can embrace with curiosity the moment to come after fully knowing the moment within the present. The silent wave of energy, initiated by the friction of wind on the initial water molecules, travels from water molecule to molecule; this is equivalent to our intention in each moment of action and thought. By being present in each moment, we have the opportunity to act with proper intention in our relationships as opposed to react reflexively or impulsively. By choosing to act and think with *right* intention, we can transfer energy from one moment to the other, thereby initiating a wave of positive energy. Like the ritual of the wave performed within the football stadium, this positive intention and energy circulates and can come back to us.

Image © rSnapshotPhotos, 2014. Used under license from Shutterstock, Inc.

What is *Right* Intention within the Context of Relationships?

Ideal intention derives from having wisdom and understanding, ethical conduct, and a mindful focus and purpose. Wisdom involves having the proper perspective or outlook on life and relationships. From a mindfulness perspective, wisdom entails accepting and understanding that every action (e.g., speech, thought, and behavior) has a result or subsequent reaction. Wholesome actions will cause results or effects of this ilk, while unwholesome acts will cause results and effects of a corresponding nature. Wisdom also entails understanding and accepting that everything that rises will cease; all things and beings that come to be are impermanent—this includes all thoughts, feelings, desires, and sensations. We tend to crave and cling onto those things and individuals who brought pleasure once but are no longer present (*Attraction*). We also avoid those things or individuals who brought some negative feeling which we wish not to know in the present (*Aversion*). Both attraction and aversion are forms of attachment to impermanent things, a refusal to recognize impermanence. This refusal equates to ignorance, the opposite of wisdom. Choosing to remain ignorant leads to suffering and unhappiness. Ignorance is not accepting that unwholesome and wholesome actions will produce results in kind. Many of us may not want to be aware of this fact because it makes it easier for us to act in ways that satisfy cravings but ultimately lead us or others to suffer because what we ultimately seek will not be obtainable or permanent. Wisdom then involves having sustained focus on knowing what to promulgate (wholesome thoughts and actions) and from what to abstain (unwholesome thoughts and actions).

With wisdom, confusion, and conflict over how to conduct oneself in terms of speech, action, and choice of livelihood become clear and not obfuscated by ignorance. Though it may seem patronizing or moralistic to preach proper speech and actions, our choices of speech and action toward others does have an impact on ourselves as well as others. Adopting ideal speech and action leads to reduced stress and suffering. Simple choices such as abstaining from lying or divisive or abusive speech can influence our relationships tremendously, and also influence how others ultimately relate to us. Henry Thoreau and Mahatma Gandhi are prime examples of individuals who demonstrated how proper speech and actions in the context of adverse situations can result in powerful shifts within dysfunctional systems. If we were to respond to an agitated, upset, and angry partner with soothing and affectionate words, with a polite and pleasing demeanor, we may help the other person and the situation reach resolution while understanding our partner better, even if maintaining divergent opinions or perspectives. Reacting with anger and responding in kind will not help either party find resolution or feel more connected to each other despite disagreement in perspectives. The distance between the two positions should ideally serve as an opportunity to know the other—by remaining mindful within such interactions allows us instead to change the chain of unwholesome actions. Being able to do this, of course, requires skills to be aware, accept, and tolerate our own feelings, thoughts, and sensations while being subjected to another's anger or disappointment. In essence, we should respond to others as we would have others respond to us when we are suffering or hurting.

When we accept that we are ultimately all interconnected, e.g., within the context of the relationship dyad, the whole relationship unit becomes liberated from ignorance. Thus, helping the other person overcome the hindrance of *ill-will*, for example, may be viewed by the struggling individual as having compassion. As we have mentioned, having compassion for others is also a way of having compassion toward ourselves. If we view the other person as being hindered from being present in the moment, we may be more tolerant and patient. Knowing that the words, feelings, and even intent of the other in one moment will not be the same in a new moment may also help us maintain greater capacity for mental equanimity.

Image © Curioso, 2014. Used under license from Shutterstock, Inc.

In other words, having faith that what is said in the heat of anger will not be words used two days later when you and your partner process the same issue in calmer states.

Our choices in terms of livelihood also have an influence on how the world and humanity manifests. Wholesome intention prevents the spread of negative or harmful energy within our larger ecosystem. Determining what livelihoods are wholesome and which are unwholesome are subject to one's religious and cultural beliefs. Despite this relativity, slave trading or manufacturing and selling of addictive substances may be more readily accepted as promulgating negative energy and intention; these acts harbor ill-intention, noncompassion. These livelihoods bring us further away from compassion and acceptance that all living creatures are interconnected. Thus, the decision to pursue or not purse a particular livelihood must include consideration of the intention behind the choice. The decision we make has significance and meaning not only to our lives but also to the system at large.

There must be a persistent commitment to make effort to abandon harmful thoughts, words, and deeds. We must maintain right awareness, memory, and attention of all aspects of experience in each moment by keeping the mind alert to experiences that affect our body and mind. In other words, we must not forget wisdom and ideal conduct and succumb to hindrances, when we are in conflict with our desires. While walking the right path involves acknowledging and accepting one will have desires, the right path requires that our actions and choices be determined by right (wholesome) intention. In such a way, killing a wounded deer suffering on the side of the road that will not live is an act of compassion, not for the action itself but for the intention behind the action.

The Role of Mindfulness and Self-Compassion in Managing Autonomic Thought Patterns

As previously noted, our thoughts and their emotional byproducts are deeply ingrained by our past social experiences, our social conditioning, and the relationships we had with our caregivers when we were

Image © John C. Hooten, 2014. Used under license from Shutterstock, Inc.

children. Therefore, habitual thought patterns can be very hard to change despite even the most sincere efforts to do so. Most of us have experienced attempts to change an unwanted behavior or habit but, to our disappointment, realize that the desire to do so is not enough to break this pattern.

What we can change, however, is how we relate to our thoughts so that our thoughts are not the primary determinant of how we conduct ourselves in relationships with others. Rather than relying on ever-changing thought patterns to determine our actions, acting in accordance with our own set of self-prescribed values is a more stable alternative. If we can view our thoughts as passing events rather than as inherent aspects of who we are or unquestionable reflections on reality,[28] we allow ourselves greater freedom to choose values-oriented actions—in that regard the practice of mindfulness can help us defuse from thoughts so that we can more consistently act in ways that are congruent with our values. To defuse in this context means to decrease our fusion with or decrease the absolute believability of thoughts.[29,30,31]

Yet, when we defuse from our thinking and develop greater awareness of our ruminative thought patterns, it is inevitable to encounter distressing thoughts that were previously being avoided or which we were perhaps unaware of at all. However, efforts to control or push away these distressing thoughts

Image © Sanjay Deva, 2014. Used under license from Shutterstock, Inc.

once they are recognized can actually make the mind more restless. On the other hand, when we allow all thoughts to come and go as simply passing events with an attitude of self-compassion, less authority is given to such thoughts, thus limiting their ability to control our actions.

While compassion is an emotional response of caring and kindness to the difficulties of others, self-compassion is caring and kindness directed toward ourselves.[32] Since the five hindrances to mindfulness that were previously discussed are obstacles for every person who attempts to be mindful, self-compassion is a potent antidote to prevent our attention from being consumed by self-criticism and not in the present moment—therefore, a significant level of self-compassion is needed to practice mindfulness successfully and self-compassion is a key mechanism for how mindfulness may reduce stress and cognitive reactivity.[33]

In order to gain greater self-compassion, compassion-related meditative practices can be utilized. Loving-kindness meditation is one such practice in which a person silently directs a series of compassion-related phrases toward visualizations in the mind of oneself and other people[34]—however, loving-kindness meditation is not merely a detached repetition of phrases but is an approach to mindfully witness our thought patterns when given a compassion-related task and to nonjudgmentally observe what is preventing us from more positively perceiving ourselves and other people. Once the thought patterns that are holding us back are observed with self-compassion, there is the potential for these thought patterns to lose their perceived validity and impetus to fuel actions that we might later regret.

As described throughout this chapter, misperception is an unavoidable trait of being human. Mark Twain poignantly captures this aspect of the human condition in his quote, "My life has been a series of tragedies; most of them never happened."[35] Thus, when we consider that all of us are fallible to believe our negative thinking patterns and misperceive situations from the deceptions of our own minds, our most skillful default response should be greater compassion for ourselves and compassion for others. This makes sense when also considering that even the word compassion is rooted in the Latin phrase, *cum patior*, meaning to suffer or stand in solidarity with another person.[36]

Image © Krasimira Nevenova, 2014. Used under license from Shutterstock, Inc.

From a scientific perspective, it has been found that intentionally cultivating self-compassion stimulates the same parts of the brain associated with feeling compassion for others.[37] In a study of 93 participants, even a 7-minute loving-kindness meditation practice demonstrated significant effects on the positive feelings that a person may have even toward neutral strangers.[38] In a randomized control trial of the 8-week Mindful Self-Compassion Program, which includes loving-kindness meditation, participants demonstrated a significant increase in self-compassion, mindfulness, and life satisfaction as well as compassion for others, when compared with control subjects. These changes were maintained at both the six months and one-year follow-up testing phases.[32]

Compassion and the Ecological Perspective

When building from self-compassion to compassion for others, there also lies the potential for a more universal sense of compassion for all living things and the planet as a whole. In ancient Chinese literature, there is a mythical description of a large net, known as *Indra's Net*, which vividly depicts this concept.[39] *Indra's Net* is described as comprising mirror-like jewels at the many locations where the ropes of the net intersect. Each jewel contains the reflection of all of the other jewels embedded within the net. The individual quality of any one jewel manifests into the collective reflection of all the other jewels. Metaphorically, every person is a jewel within this universal net of living things. What each person resonates through their intention of either compassion or ill-will toward themselves and toward others is reflected within all of the jewels of the net.

Along similar lines, ecopsychology is the study of the reciprocal links between the health of the physical environment, humans, and all other living creatures.[40] Ecopsychology recognizes that humans and all components of the natural world are interconnected pieces and equally necessary to maintain balance within an interdependent ecosystem. From an ecopsychological perspective, intentionally harming any aspect of the ecosystem ripples through all aspects of the ecosystem like an ocean wave impacts the currents of all connected bodies of water and like the reflections of the jewels that ricochet across Indra's Net.

Image © Nagy-Bagoly Arpad, 2014. Used under license from Shutterstock, Inc.

With a greater sense of inner and outer awareness fostered through mindfulness we can recognize the synergistic connections between ourselves, our relationships, and of our planet.[41] Meditation teacher, Thich Nhat Hanh points out *"The flower cannot exist by itself alone; it has to inter-be with soil, rain, weeds and insects. There is no being; there is only inter-being."*[42] Likewise, in the practice of mindful eating, it is suggested that before consuming one's food to consider where the food might have come from, how it was grown or made, the people who labored to produce this food, and the impact that natural elements like sunshine and rain had on the production of this food, which will nourish our bodies so that we can take action in the world.[43] When considering these interconnections before eating, there is a greater likelihood to have a profound sense of gratitude for the food we will be consuming. Yet with greater awareness, comes greater responsibility and therefore, it should not be surprising that mindfulness is associated with greater ecologically-responsible behavior.[44,45]

While modern technology, news media, and global consumerism have made our interpersonal connections undeniably apparent, the importance of our interconnections still might not be a primary focus for many people—therefore, rather than relying on an outer technology to guide us, it is best to start with the inner technology of mindfulness so that we may be inclined to develop healthy relationships across personal, interpersonal, and ecological domains for our own benefit, the benefit of others, and for the benefit of generations to follow. In that regard, as mindfulness begins to undo what Einstein called our "optical delusion of consciousness," we all have the potential to recognize that these domains were never actually separate after all.[46]

References

1. Einstein, A., *The New Quotable Einstein.* Edited by Calaprice A. Princeton, NJ: Princeton University Press, 2005.

2. Harris, R., "Through Bracing Your Demons: An Overview of Acceptance and Commitment Therapy," *Psychotherapy in Australia* 12 no. (4) (2006): 2–8.

3. Kessler, R. C., Berglund, P., Demler, O., Jin, R., Merikangas, K. R., & Walters, E. E., "Lifetime Prevalence and Age-of-onset Distributions of DSM-IV Disorders in the National Comorbidity Survey Replication: Erratum," *Archives of General Psychiatry* 62 no. (7) (2005): 768.

4. Kessler, R. C., Berglund, P., Demler, O., Jin, R., Koretz, D., Merikangas, K. R., & Wang P. S., "The Epidemiology of Major Depressive Disorder: Results from the National Comorbidity Survey Replication (NCS-R)," *Journal of the American Medical Association* 289 no. (23) (2003): 3095–4105.

5. Davies, T., "ABC of Mental Health," *British Medical Journal* 314 (1997): 1536–39.

6. Kessler, R. C., McGonagle, K. A., Zhao, S., Nelson, C. B., Hughes, M., Eshleman, S., Kendler, K. S., "Lifetime and 12-month Prevalence of DSM III-R: Psychiatric Disorders in the United States," *Archives of General Psychiatry* 51 (1994): 8–19.

7. Sartre, J., *Being and Nothingness*. Translated by Hazel E. Barnes. New York: Philosophical Library, 1948.

8. Camus, A., *The Myth of Sisyphus and Other Essays*. New York: Alfred A. Knopf, 1955.

9. Tennyson, A., *In Memoriam*, 1850/2014. Accessed from http://classiclit.about.com/library/ bl-etexts/atennyson/bl-aten-memoriam.htm.

10. Fairbairn, R. D., "Reevaluating Some Basic Concepts." In *From Instinct to Self edited by* D. E. Scharff & E. F. Birtles (129–38). Northvale, NJ: Jason Aronson, Inc., 1995.

11. Bowlby J., *Attachment and Loss, vol. 1, 2nd ed.* New York: Basic Books, 1969/1999.

12. Harlow, H. F. & Zimmermann, R. R., "The Development of Affectional Responses in Infant Monkeys," *Proceedings of the American Philosophical Society* 102 (1958): 501–09.

13. Spitz, R. A., "Hospitalism: An Inquiry into the Genesis of Psychiatric Conditions in Early Childhood," *The Psychoanalytic Study of the Child* 1 (1945): 53–74.

14. Freud, S., *Civilization and its Discontents*. New York, NY: W.W. Norton & Co, 1962.

15. Uchino, B. N., *Social Support and Physical Health: Understanding the Health Consequences of Our Relationships*. New Haven, CT: Yale University Press, 2004.

16. De Vogli, R., Chandola, T., & Marmot, M. G., "Negative Aspects of Close Relationships and Heart Disease," *Archives of Internal Medicine* 167 (2007): 1951–57. doi:10.1001/archinte.167.18.1951.

17. Holt-Lunstad, J., Smith, T. B., & Layton, B., "Social Relationships and Mortality: A Meta-analysis," *PLoS Medicine* 7 (2010): e1000316. doi:10.1371/journal.pmed.1000316.

18. Graham, J. E., Glaser, R., Loving, T. J., Malarkey, W. B., Stowell, J. R., & Kiecolt-Glaser, J. K., "Cognitive Word Use During Marital Conflict Attenuates Increases in Inflammatory Cytokines," *Health Psychology* 28 (2009): 621–30. doi:10.1037/a0015208.

19. Uchino, B. N., Cawthon R. M., Smith T. W., Light K. C., McKenzie J., & Carlisle , M., "Social Relationships and Health: Is Feeling Positive, Negative, or Both (Ambivalent) About Your Social Ties Related to Telomeres?" *Health Psychology* 31 no. (6) (2012): 789–96. doi: 10.1037/a0026836.

20. Cawthon, R. M., Smith, K. R., O'Brien, E., Sivatchenko, A., & Kerber, R. A., "Association Between Telomere Length in Blood and Mortality in People Aged 60 Years or Older," *Lancet* 361 (2003): 393–95. doi:10.1016/S0140-6736(03)123847.

21. Cordova, J. V., Gee, C. P., & Warren, L. Z., Emotional Skillfulness in Marriage: Intimacy as Mediator of Relationship Between Emotional Skillfulness and Marital Satisfaction," *Journal of Social and Clinical Psychology* 24 no. (2) (2005): 218–35.

22. Wachs, K., & Cordova, J. V., "Mindful Relating: Exploring Mindfulness and Emotion Repertoires in Intimate Relationships," *Journal of Marital and Family Therapy* 33 (2007): 464–81. doi:10.1111/j.1752– 0606.2007.00032x.

23. Hayes, S. C., Wilson, K. D., Gifford, E. V., Follette, V. M., & Strosahl, K., "Emotional Avoidance and Behavioral Disorders: A Functional Dimensional Approach to Diagnosis and Treatment," *Journal of Consulting and Clinical Psychology* 64 (1996): 1152–68.

24. Davidson, R. J., Kabat-Zinn, J., Schumacher, J., Rosenkranz, M., Muller, D., Santorelli, S. F., [. . .] & Sheridan, J. F., "Alterations in Brain and Immune Function Produced by Mindfulness Meditation," *Psychosomatic Medicine* 65 (2003): 564–70.

25. Pagnoni, G. & Cekic, M., "Age Effects on Gray Matter Volume and Attentional Performance in Zen Meditation," *Neurobiology of Aging* 28 (2007): 1623–27.

26. Bowen S., Witkiewitz K., Dillworth T. M., Chawla N., Simpson T. L., Ostafin B. D., [. . .] & Marlatt G. A., "Mindfulness Meditation and Substance Use in An Incarcerated Population," *Psychology of Addictive Behaviors* 20 (2006): 343–47.

27. Chiesa, A., & Serretti, A., "A Systematic Review of Neurobiological and Clinical Features of Mindfulness Meditations," *Psychological Medicine* 40 (2010): 1239–52. doi:10.1017/S0033291709991747.

28. Bishop, S. R., Lau, M., Shapiro, S., Carlson, L., Anderson, N. D., Carmody, J., [. . .] Devins, G., "Mindfulness: A Proposed Operational Definition," *Clinical Psychology: Science and Practice* 11 (2004): 230–41.

29. Hayes, S. C., Luoma, J. B., Bond, F. W., Masuda, A., & Lillis, J., "Acceptance and Commitment Therapy: Model, Processes and Outcomes," *Behaviour Research & Therapy* 44 (2006): 1–25.

30. Hayes, S. C., & Shenk, C., "Operationalizing Mindfulness Without Unnecessary Attachments," *Clinical & Psychological Science* 11 (2004): 249–54.

31. Masuda, A., Hayes, S. C., Sackett, C. F., & Twohig, M. P., "Cognitive Defusion and Self-relevant Negative Thoughts: Examining the Impact of a Ninety-year Old Technique," *Behaviour Research and Therapy* 42 (2004): 477–85.

32. Neff, K. D., & Germer, C. K., "A Pilot Study and Randomized Controlled Trial of the Mindful Self-compassion Program," *Journal of Clinical Psychology* 69 no. (1) (2013): 28–44. doi:10.1002/jclp.21923.

33. Kuyken, W., Dalgleish, T., Watkins, E., Holden, E., White, K., Taylor, R. S., [. . .] & Teasdale, J. D., "How Does Mindfulness-based Cognitive Therapy Work?,"*Behaviour Research and Therapy* 48 no. (11) (2010): 1105–12. doi:10.1016/j.brat.2010.08.003.

34. Germer, C. K., *The Mindful Path to Self-compassion: Freeing Yourself from Destructive Thoughts and Emotions.* New York, NY: The Guilford Press, 2009.

35. Carlson, L. E. & Speca, M., *Mindfulness-based Cancer Recovery.* Oakland, CA: New Harbinger, 2010.

36. Staren, E. D., "Compassion and Communication in Cancer Care," *The American Journal of Surgery* 192 (2006): 411–15.

37. Longe, O., Maratos, F. A., Gilbert, P., Evans, G., Volker, F., Rockliff, H., & Rippon, G., "Having a Word with Yourself: Neural Correlates of Self-criticism and Self-reassurance," *Neuroimage* 49 no. (2) (2010): 1849–56. doi:10.1016/j.neuroimage.2009.09.019.

38. Hutcherson, C. A., Seppala, E. M., & Gross, J. J., "Loving-kindness Meditation Increases Social Connectedness," *Emotion* 8 no. (5) (2008): 720–24. doi:10.1037/a0013237.

39. Kaza, S., "Western Buddhist Motivations for Vegetarianism," *World Views: Environment, Culture, Religion* 9 no. (3) (2005): 385–411. doi:10.1163/156853505774841650.

40. Conn, S., "Living in the Earth: Ecopsychology, Health and Psychotherapy," *The Humanistic Psychologist* 26 no. (1) (1998): 179–98. doi:10.1080/08873267.1998.9976972.

41. Kabat-Zinn, J., *Coming to Our Senses: Healing Ourselves and the World Through Mindfulness.* New York, NY: Hyperion, 2005.

42. Hanh, T. N., *No Death, No Fear: Comforting Wisdom for Life.* New York, NY: Penguin Group, 2002.

43. Kabat-Zinn, J., *Full Catastrophe Living: Using the Wisdom of Your Body and Mind to Face Stress, Pain, and Illness.* New York, NY: Bantam, 1999.

44. Amel, E. L., Manning, C. M., & Scott, B. A., "Mindfulness and Sustainable Behavior: Pondering Attention and Awareness as Means for Increasing Green Behavior," *Ecopsychology* 1 no. (1) (2009): 14–25.

45. Brown, K. W., & Kasser, T., "Are Psychological and Ecological Well-being Compatible?: The Role of Values, Mindfulness, and Lifestyle," *Social Indicators Research* 74 no. (2) (2005): 349–68. doi:10.1007/s11205-004-8207-8.

46. Kabat-Zinn, J., *Lifescape:* On *Guided Mindfuness Mediation, Series 3* [CD]. Boulder, CO: Sounds True, 2012.

CHAPTER 7 WORKSHEET

Questions

1. Explain how mindfulness helps improve marital adjustment and satisfaction.

2. Choose either the metaphor of the wave or the analogy of Indra's net and articulate its relevance to the concept of mindfulness.

3. There are five distinct types of distraction that hinder our ability to develop and maintain mindfulness. List and define each hindrance.

4. Why does it matter whether we make an effort to abandon harmful thoughts, words, and deeds?

5. How does self-compassion relate to mindfulness?

6. Describe how the concept of "inter-being" relates to ecopsychology.

Activities

1. Find a quiet space where you will not be disturbed for the next 10 minutes. Find a comfortable place to sit and place a blank piece of paper and pencil next to you. Close your eyes and breathe normally. Let your mind drift until you forget you are doing this exercise. When you realize that you have drifted, bring your attention back to the exercise and note immediately where your mind had drifted. Write on the paper next to you where your mind had most recently drifted. Write down what ever you like about the thoughts, memory, or feelings. Note if you were experiencing tension anywhere in your body associated with the thoughts or memories. Identify which of the five hindrances underlie your experience. For example, did it involve sensual desire, doubt, fear, or guilt?

2. Sit for a moment in a quiet space and think back to your childhood. Allow your mind to wonder freely through your past memories. If initially this is difficult for you, be patient and do not condemn yourself or the exercise. After some time, locate a memory that you do not wish to focus on. Allow yourself to continue to focus on it and to examine it. It should be a memory in which you experience a negative emotion or feeling, one on which you would not normally want to stay focused. Identify what is the central feeling that emerges for you out of this memory. Describe the experience and the feeling and whether or not it was difficult for you to remain focused on the memory.

3. Sit comfortably in a chair in an upright position but also relaxed. Close your eyes and focus on your inhalations and exhalations as two distinct events in the breath cycle. Don't try to breathe in any special way; simply feel your breath somewhere in your body. When thoughts arise, which they will, just note that *a thought* has arisen, not what the thought was about but simply that it was *a thought*, and then without self-criticism that you are no longer paying attention to your breath, gently redirect your attention back to your breathing.

   After you feel a little more centered and less distracted than when you began, bring up an image in your mind of a person who has loved or supported you in your life. This might be a parent, grandparent, coach, teacher, or friend. This could also be someone who you've never met but who inspires you. With the image of this person in your attention, silently repeat the following phrases in your mind directed at that person:

May you be safe
May you be happy
May you be healthy
May you live with ease

   The key is to *try* to truly mean and feel what these phrases are saying. Your mind might become very resistant to this exercise, tell you a story about why this is silly, or wander into thinking about something else, but when it does simply redirect your attention back to the image and the phrases. Try this for about 3 minutes, gently bringing your attention back to the image and phrases each time. Next, bring up an image of yourself in your mind. It might even be helpful to bring up an image of yourself as a young child. With that image secure in your attention, now silently repeat the following phrases in your mind directed at that image of yourself:

May I be safe
May I be happy
May I be healthy
May I live with ease

Like before, try to really mean and feel what you are saying. If you notice any resistance in your body or your mind to directing these phrases at yourself, simply note whatever your experience is without self-judgment or self-criticism but with self-compassion simply redirect your attention back to your image of yourself and the phrases. Try this for about 3 more minutes. Lastly, for another minute drop all images and return your attention only to sensations of breathing again and then gently open your eyes.

At this point, you might wish to write down or simply reflect upon what came up in your body and mind when you tried to send these phrases and feelings of loving-kindness to another person and to yourself. Make sure you are only making note of what happened in your experience rather than judging yourself harshly for perhaps not being able to stick with instructions at any point. Just noticing when your attention got distracted is in fact the practice of mindfulness just as much as noticing when your attention stayed on the breath or perhaps on the images and phrases.

4. Find a comfortable place to sit outside. This might be a park bench, or on your patio, or even perhaps under a tree. Like the previous meditation, start by feeling your breathing cycle somewhere in your body, feeling each unique inhalation and exhalation. When your attention drifts into thinking, simply note that the experience is happening and then gently redirect your attention back to the sensations of your breathing. Now shift your attention to something happening in nature. This might be feeling of the breeze or the sunlight or the sound of birds or crickets chirping. Whatever it is, pick only one thing and try to fully experience it as interacts with your senses.

When your attention wanders into other aspects that are happening in nature or perhaps into a thought in the mind, notice what has happened and without self-criticism gently redirect your attention to your originally chosen aspect of nature. With your attention on this aspect of nature, try to fully experience all of its subtleties and dimensions, notice how this aspect of nature changes moment-by-moment and how or if these changes impact the sensations in your body. Try this exercise for at least 5 minutes and then gently open your eyes. Throughout the rest of the day, simply notice if your body and mind feels any different than it did before this exercise.

MINDFUL AWARENESS REFLECTION JOURNAL

4 Step **MAC** Guide

Choose one mindful experience as you begin your reflection.

Empathically Acknowledge

Describe your experience

_____

_____

_____

Intentional Attention

Describe what you noticed

Breath
Body
Emotions
Thoughts
Senses

Accept Without Judgment

Describe judgment; acceptance

_____

_____

_____

Willingly Choose

Intention/willingness; new perspective

_____

_____

_____

Mindful Mac Meditation

Describe your meditation experiences. What did you learn?

_____

_____

_____

Name: _____   Date: _____

CHAPTER CRITICAL THINKING AND ACTIVITY JOURNAL

This is an opportunity for you to fully describe your thoughts, opinions and experience following the reading and activities.

The most important information/key concepts we need to understand from these chapters are:

_____

_____

_____

_____

How can I use the information in the chapters to help me with my daily mindfulness practice?

_____

_____

_____

_____

In what ways will the material learned in these chapters help me manage my stress more effectively?

_____

_____

_____

_____

What are your thoughts and feedback regarding the information and activities for each chapter?

_____

_____

_____

_____

CHAPTER EIGHT

EPILOGUE: HAPPINESS IS BLISS
Paying It Forward

By Maria Napoli

"When you arise in the morning,
think of what a precious privilege it is to be alive—
to breathe, to think, to enjoy, to love—
then make that day count!"

Steve Marabolli[1]

Image © aaron belford, 2014. Used under license from Shutterstock, Inc.

As you come to the end of *Beyond Stress: Strategies for Blissful Living*, you have had time to reflect upon your life and make decisions about the changes you would like to make, how you can make those changes, and what the future can bring. Mindfully embarking upon your life's path, you may realize that the prize is not in reaching the end goal, but in the experiences you encounter along the journey. What you do in each step of your life from birth to older adulthood impacts the next milestone. All of the above can offer you the one thing you strive for: *happiness.* People have many kinds of ideas about what brings happiness. Yet we find that, overall, being connected to ourselves and to others is a direct route to being happy.

"Happiness held is the seed; happiness shared is the flower."

—Author Unknown[2]

Happiness and Relationships

First and foremost, those of us who have close relationships, regardless of how many (the key here is close, intimate relationships), are happier than those who are isolated or alone. Sharing with others, feelings, activities, and offering support, determine the quality of happy relationships. College students who scored the highest on a survey of personal happiness had fewer signs of depression—not only "strong ties to friends and family but also a commitment to spending time with them."[3] Being connected is the most important ingredient in our relationships. People do not need a plethora of relationships to be happy. Having one close relationship with a willingness to share feelings and personal issues is important. Without those ingredients, people would still be lonely in those relationships.[4] Simply stated, our connection to others by sharing and giving is essential to happiness.

Image © Vitalinka, 2014. Used under license from Shutterstock, Inc.

"Happiness is like a kiss . . . you must share it to enjoy it."

—Bernard Meltzer[5]

In addition to giving and sharing with our friends and family, it has been shown that giving to others through volunteering increases our happiness; it is difficult to argue with the benefits of loving kindness. People who care for others have been found to have less depression and higher life satisfaction—they are more protected from disease and even death.[6] As we age, older adults can become more isolated, particularly as they lose the ones they love. Loneliness and depression can be difficult for older adults who may begin to lose their mobility and as their children move away for employment. Finding ways to connect with others may not only increase happiness, but also add to longevity. Older volunteers have been found to volunteer simply to offer their services and in turn feel more satisfaction than those who volunteer for external purposes, such as students who volunteer in order to get into a prestigious college.[7] Our *intention* of how we engage in relationships has the biggest impact on our happiness.

"Can't Buy Me Love"

Many of us may dream of winning the lottery—we fantasize about how happy we can be if only we won those million dollars. You are not alone in such a fantasy, particularly when the pot of money grows rapidly into the millions, almost overnight. Here's an interesting fact about lottery winners and life-changing events in regard to happiness: people who have won the lottery report similar levels of happiness to those who have been paralyzed within one year following this life-changing event! We develop behavioral patterns throughout our lives—it is no surprise that when we experience a major life-changing event, people become adjusted to the change of life whether it is a happy change or an unhappy change, and then it levels out.[8] We have all heard the expression "money cannot buy happiness," yet knowing that only *we can create* happiness with our actions may be news to some.

Image © Oksana Kuzmina, 2014. Used under license from Shutterstock, Inc.

"The joy that isn't shared dies young."
—Anne Sexton[9]

There are many decisions that contribute to college students deciding upon a career. Too often, the career that offers the most money is the one chosen and supported by parents. In fact, I have heard many students say, "I have chosen this major because my parents do not approve of the one I'm passionate about because it does not pay enough." Many people find themselves in jobs and careers that pay the big bucks—they are able to buy the things they thought would make them happy only to find out they are not any happier. Research has found that money cannot buy happiness. A study of lawyers who earned much lower incomes found that service lawyers were happier than money lawyers, who earned higher incomes. The service lawyers experienced more well-being and less negative affect—they also drank less often.[10]

In addition to reaping the benefits of serving others first instead of being concerned about the amount of money we earn, it is actually how we spend our money that contributes to our happiness. When students were given money and the choice to either spend it on others or themselves, those who spent it on others reported higher happiness scores.[11] As we discussed earlier, the significance of sharing in our relationships offered the most happiness. The same could be said with our money—sharing it brings us more joy than spending it on ourselves. We get more happiness from our experiences than from the material things we acquire.[12]

Giving Is Contagious

Does surrounding ourselves with people who "give" increase our propensity to "pay it forward"? Think about those times when you shared a good deed, a positive thought, or gave a heartfelt gift. Now think about what it felt like to buy something for yourself. The difference between these two acts is the joy shared between two people, a connection of joy and gratitude, rather than joy felt by an individual. When we are able to bring joy to another person and witness that joy, it is bliss simply because it is shared.

Image © Maisna, 2014. Used under license from Shutterstock, Inc.

An interesting experiment with Capuchin monkeys and four-year-old children found that when the monkey or child experienced a positive outcome from a donation in a game, the receiver of that donation then offered a positive outcome to another member of their social group. When either the Capuchin monkey or child experienced a negative outcome, they offered a negative outcome to a member of their social group. These results show that the giving behavior of both children and monkeys can be attributed to prior received outcomes and paid both positive and negative behavior forward in kind.[13] One might say based on this study that, "you give what you get."

Did you know people are able to detect happiness in another person who is giving, even when they are not involved in the experience? Participants in a study were asked to purchase a goody bag, for either themselves, or a sick child. Those who spent the money on others were happier. Interestingly, strangers not involved in the experiment, but observing from nearby, were able to detect the emotion of those participants![14] Students who carried out five 'random acts of kindness' of their choice reported higher levels of happiness than the students in a control group.

Image © jocic, 2014. Used under license from Shutterstock, Inc.

"If every grateful action were suddenly eliminated, society would crumble"
—(Georg Simmel)[15]

Research has also found that individuals experience more happiness when an act of kindness is done for someone we know versus a stranger and that varying the types of kindness offers more happiness to the giver.[16] For example, thanking a friend for their support by taking them to dinner will bring more happiness than paying the toll for the person behind you, even though happiness is derived in both situations. Paying it forward can be contagious. A report of "pay it forward" chains, where one person at a coffee drive through paid for the car behind it, set off a chain of paying it forward of 226 customers.[17] Paying it forward has been embraced nationally in Australia by designating an annual Pay It Forward Day in 2007, which is now celebrated worldwide each year on April 28th. It is reported that 700 million volunteer hours are donated each year to help the community during the International Pay It Forward Day. Each year on April 28th people from all over the world are passing on their generosity[18] and a study of Chinese undergraduate students who were asked "what is happiness?" found that, "Happiness can be achieved provided that one has the following abilities: (a) the wisdom of discovery; (b) the wisdom of contentment and gratitude; (c) the wisdom of giving; and (d) the wisdom of self-cultivation."[19(pl. 407)] The expression, "You cannot have it unless you give it away," may have merit based on the benefits reaped from sharing and giving.

Image © Helder Almeida, 2014. Used under license from Shutterstock, Inc.

"Cultivate the habit of being grateful for every good thing that comes to you, and to give thanks continuously. And because all things have contributed to your advancement, you should include all things in your gratitude."

—Ralph Waldo Emerson[20]

Gratitude Is the Best Attitude

Happiness is also achieved when one experiences gratitude. Emmons notes "Gratitude is the feeling that occurs when a person attributes a benefit they have received from another."[21] We know that emotions can affect our physical body. For example, the feeling of being in love can accelerate our heart rate, stimulate abdominal flutters, and increase energy. Have you ever considered that giving to others could affect your physical state? People receive physical sensations of muscle relaxation when they are grateful.[22] People who are grateful report being more agreeable and less narcissistic compared with less grateful people and report being happier.[23] Research has shown that receiving help from others resulted in a desire to help others. When adults talk and write about what they are grateful for, it increases their happiness as well as savoring the smallest pleasures.[24] One might conclude that being grateful may encourage people to do something good for another, and can have long lasting benefits to society as people "pay it forward' with gratitude.

"Making money isn't hard in itself... What's hard is to earn it doing something worth devoting one's life to."
—Carlos Ruiz Zafon, The Shadow of the Wind[25]

Living mindfully is one of the best predictors to happiness and gratitude. Being in the moment without judgment disposes of the "waste" we could accumulate, hence, interfering with our potential to move forward, create change and see life with a fresh outlook. People who scored high on mindfulness had high self-compassion and well-being—the more mindful the caregiver of mentally ill patients the happier the patient.[26] When we approach life mindfully, we experience each moment more fully.

It is no surprise that being stuck in negative thinking affects our psychological and physical health. We learned in earlier chapters that moving out of fight or flight and into a state of homeostasis, igniting the parasympathetic nervous system, is a route toward healing. One way to get there mindfully is by having an optimistic attitude. As you begin to find ways to ignite your parasympathetic nervous system and enjoy the benefits of rest and relaxation, offer a family member who is experiencing stress an opportunity for a massage, to babysit, or take charge of a chore to relieve their burden. Research has found that when we are optimistic, we improve the immune system and prevent chronic disease as well as being a protector against depression and heart disease,[27, 28] and prevention of chronic illness.[29, 30] Yes, it makes perfect sense to move out of fight or flight and give those immune soldiers some power! Mindfully letting go of judgments will move us from being stuck and propel us forward, paving the road for happiness.

Each chapter in *Beyond Stress: Strategies for Blissful Living* gives you an opportunity to plant seeds for transformation. In order to truly achieve happiness, the act of "paying it forward" must be an integral part of your life. We all know the story of *A Christmas Carol* and how the character Scrooge was transformed from a miser to a man of generosity. One could feel the emotional and physical changes of the character when he experienced happiness over misery. Most of us have heard, "It's better to give than receive"; yet quantifying this cliché through research has become popular through positive psychology.

Now that you have mindfully read the chapters, experienced the activities, and practiced mindful meditation, you hopefully have become more aware of your strengths and personal assets. Take the various VIA signature strengths tests below and find out more about yourself. You will increase your happiness when you become in tune with and begin to utilize your strengths. Students who used the signature strengths were found to be successful in reaching their goals and improving their well-being,[31] and those who possessed hope, zest, gratitude, love, and curiosity had a stronger link to life satisfaction.[32]

We have come full circle in our journey—mindfully acknowledging, paying attention to, and letting go of judgments, and making choices about our experiences. What a wonderful world we can create if we mindfully perform random acts of kindness. As we change our nutritional patterns to live a healthier life, think about ways to contribute to others. For example, joining a community garden, offering information to a friend about healthy eating, or going grocery shopping with them. As you begin to find ways to ignite your parasympathetic nervous system and enjoy the benefits of rest and relaxation, offer a family member who is experiencing stress an opportunity for a massage, to babysit, or take charge of a chore to relieve their burden. The next time you are having a conversation with your friend, partner, or family member, mindfully listen without interrupting, be silent until that person has stopped talking, and offer nonjudgmental attention. Last but not least, quiet your mind and listen to the information offered through your instincts and intuition and reap the benefits of paying attention to your "gut." You are on the road to living a blissful life—enjoy it and share it with everyone you encounter!

References

1. http://www.goodreads.com/quotes/tag/gratitude.
2. http://www.pursuit-of-happiness.org/science-of-happiness/communicating/.
3. Wallis, C., The New Science of Happiness. *Time Magazine*, January 9, 2005.
4. Jackson, T., Soderlind, A., & Weiss, K. E., "Personality Traits and Quality of Relationships as Predictors of Future Loneliness Among American College Students," *Social Behavior and Personality: An International Journal* 28 no. (5) (2000): 463–70.

5. http://www.pursuit-of-happiness.org/science-of-happiness/communicating/.

6. Broadhead, W. E., Kaplan, B. H., James, S. A., Wagner, E. H., Schoenbach, V. J., Grimson, R., Heyden, S., Tibblin, G., & Gehlbach, S. H., "The Epidemiologic Evidence for a Relationship Between Social Support and Health," *American Journal of Epidemiology* 117 (1883): 521–37.

7. Kahana, E., Bhatta, T., Lovegreen, L. D., Kahana, B., & Midlarsky, E., "Altruism, Helping, and Volunteering: Pathways to Well-Being in Late Life," *Journal of Aging and Health* 25 (2013): 159–87. doi: 10.1177/0898264312469665.

8. Wargo, E., "Aiming at Happiness and Shooting Ourselves in the Foot," *APS Observer* (9) no. (16) (2011). August http://www.psychologicalscience.org/observer/getArticle.cfm?id=2188. Generation G AE, the new wave of Australians making a difference, *Get the Word Out,* April 20, 2011, 15:21 (http://www.getthewordout.com.au/20110420225/news-room/generation-g-the-new-wave-of-australians-making-a-difference.htm).

9. http://www.goodreads.com/quotes/tag/gratitude.

10. Sheldon, K., M., & Krieger, L. S., "Service Job Lawyers are Happier than Money Job Lawyers, Despite Their Lower Income," *Journal of positive Psychology* 9 no. (3) (2014): 219–26.

11. Geenen, N. Y. R., Hoheluchter, M., Langholf, V. & Walther, E., "The Beneficial Effects of Prosocial Spending on Happiness: Word Hard, Make Money, and Spend it on Others?," *Journal of Positive Psychology* 9 (3) (2014): 204–08.

12. Baucells, Manel & Sarin, Rakesh K., Achieving the Elusive Goal of Happiness, *Insight,* May 23, 2009. http://insight.iese.edu/doc.aspx?id=937&ar=18.

13. Leimgruber, K. L., Ward, A. F., Widness, J., Norton, M. I.,Olson, K. R., Gray, K., Santos, L. R., Give What you Get: Capuchin Monkeys (Cebus apella) and Four-year Old Children Pay Forward Positive and Negative Outcomes to Conspecifics *PLoS ONE* 9, no. 4 (2014): e96959. doi: 10: 1371/journal.pone.0096959.

14. Aknin, L. B., Fleerackers, A. L., & Hamlin, J. K., "Can Third-party Observers Detect the Emotional Rewards of Generous Spending?" *Journal of Positive Psychology* 9 (3) (2014): 198–203.

15. http://www.goodreads.com/quotes/tag/gratitude.

16. Svoboda, E., Pay It Forward. *Psychology Today*, July 1, 2006.

17. Matter, G., "The Science of "Paying It Forward," (2014) The *New York Times, March 14* (18) (2011) Generation G AE, the new wave of Australians making a difference, *Get the Word Out,* April 20th 15:21.

18. http://www.getthewordout.com.au/20110420225/news-room/generation-g-the-new-wave-of-australians-making-a-difference.htm.

19. Luo, Lu. "Understanding Happiness: A Look into the Chinese Folk Psychology," *Journal of Happiness Studies* 2 (2001): 407–32.

20. http://www.goodreads.com/quotes/tag/gratitude.

21. Tsang, J., "Gratitude and Prosocial Behaviour: An Experimental Test of Gratitude," *Cognition and Emotion* 20 (2006): 138–48.

22. Algoe, S. B., & Haidt, J., "Witnessing Excellence in Action: the 'other-praising' Eemotions of Elevation, Gratitude and Admiration," *Journal of Positive Psychology* 4 no. (2) (2009): 105–27.

23. Watkins, P. C, Woodward, K., Stone, T., & Kolts, R. L., "Gratitude and Happiness: Development of a Measure of Gratitude, and Relationships with Subjective Well Being," *Social Behavior and Personality* 31 no. (5) (2003): 431–52.

24. Elias, M., "Psychologist Now Know What Makes People Happy," *USA Today,* December 8, 2002.

25. http://www.goodreads.com/quotes/tag/money.

26. Carmody, J., & Baer, R. A., "Relationships Between Mindfulness Practice and Levels of Mindfulness, Medical and Psychological Symptoms and Well-being in a Mindfulness-based Stress Reduction Program," *Journal of Behavioral Medicine* 1 (2008): 23–33. doi:10.1007/s10865-007-9130-7.

27. Tindle, H. A., Chang, Y. F., Kuller, L. H., Manson, J. E., Robinson, J. G., Rosal, M. C., Siegle, G. J., & Matthews, K., A., "Optimism, Cynical Hostility, and Incident Coronary Heart Disease and Mortality in the Women's Health Initiative," *Circulation* 120 no. (8) (2009): 656–62. doi: 10.1161/ CIRCULATIONAHA.108.827642.

28. Segerstrom, S. C., & Sephton, S. E., "Optimistic Expectancies and Cell-Mediated Immunity: The Role of Positive Affect," *Psychological Science* 21 no. (3) (2014): 448–55.

29. Matthews, K. A., Raikkonen, K., Sutton-Tyrrell, K., & Kuller, L. H., "Optimistic Attitudes Protect Against Progression of Carotid Atherosclerosis in Healthy Middle-aged Women," *Psychosomatic Medicine* 66 no. (5) (2004): 640–44.

30. Kohut, M. L., Cooper, M. M., Nickolaus, M. S., Russell, D. R., & Cunnick, J. E., "Exercise and Psychosocial Factors Modulate Immunity to Influenza Vaccine in Elderly Individuals," *Journal of Gerontology* 57 (9) (2002): 557–62.

31. Liney, P. A., Nielsen, K. M., Gillett, R., & Biswas-Diener, R., "Using Signature Strengths in Pursuit of Goals: Effects on Goal Progress, Need Satisfaction, and Well-being, and Implications for Coaching Psychologists," *International Coaching Psychology Review* 5 no. (1) (2010): 6–15.

32. Park, N., Peterson, C., & Seligman, M., "Strengths of Character and Well-being," *Journal of Social and Clinical Psychology* 23 (2004): 603–19.

WORKSHEET

Activities

The following questionnaires are taken from Positive Psychology and will give you an assessment of your core strengths and levels of happiness. Enjoy!

1. **Take this happiness quiz and see how happy you are?**
   http://www.pursuit-of-happiness.org/take-the-objective-happiness-quiz/

2. VIA Signature Strengths Questionnaire
   Measures 24 Character Strengths

3. **Compassionate love Scale**
   Measures your tendency to support, help, and understand other people Source: Sprecher, S. & Fehr, B. (2005). Compassionate love for close others and humanity. Journal of Social and Personal Relationships, 22, 629-652. Used with permission of Susan Sprecher. ©2005 Susan Sprecher and Beverly Fehr
   http://www.authentichappiness.sas.upenn.edu/Entry.aspx?rurl=http://www.authentichappiness.sas.upenn.edu/tests/SameAnswers_t.aspx?id=1339

4. **Approaches to Happiness Scale**
   http://www.authentichappiness.sas.upenn.edu/Entry.aspx?rurl=http://www.authentichappiness.sas.upenn.edu/tests/SameAnswers_t.aspx?id=266

5. **General Happiness Questionnaire**
   Assesses Enduring Happiness Form Authentic Happiness, Chapter 4 - Can You Make Yourself Lastingly Happier? Questionnaire developed by Lyubomirsky & Lepper (1999). Used with permission.
   http://www.authentichappiness.sas.upenn.edu/Entry.aspx?rurl=http://www.authentichappiness.sas.upenn.edu/tests/GeneralTest_t.aspx?id=250

6. **Gratitude Journal**
   Keep a daily gratitude journal. Read it often and fill it with experiences that make you smile.

Quiz Questions:

1. Describe the benefits of gratitude.

2. What does the literature say regarding happiness?

3. What did you learn from the study of capuchin monkey and four-year-old children regarding giving?

4. What did you learn about the effects of third party observers and those who give?

5. What is the relationship between the physical and emotional outcome of giving?

6. Discuss the how relationships impact happiness.

7. Discuss how paying it forward can be contagious.

8. Can money buy happiness? Describe.

MINDFUL AWARENESS REFLECTION JOURNAL

Choose one mindful experience as you begin your reflection.

Empathically Acknowledge

Describe your experience

_____

_____

_____

Intentional Attention

Describe what you noticed

Breath
Body
Emotions
Thoughts
Senses

Accept Without Judgment

Describe judgment; acceptance

_____

_____

_____

Willingly Choose

Intention/willingness; new perspective

_____

_____

_____

Mindful Mac Meditation

Describe your meditation experiences. What did you learn?

_____

_____

_____

CHAPTER CRITICAL THINKING AND ACTIVITY JOURNAL

This is an opportunity for you to fully describe your thoughts, opinions and experience following the reading and activities.

The most important information/key concepts we need to understand from these chapters are:

_____

_____

_____

_____

How can I use the information in the chapters to help me with my daily mindfulness practice?

_____

_____

_____

_____

In what ways will the material learned in these chapters help me manage my stress more effectively?

_____

_____

_____

_____

What are your thoughts and feedback regarding the information and activities for each chapter?

_____

_____

_____

_____